Answers
to
Bible
Questions
You
Have
Asked

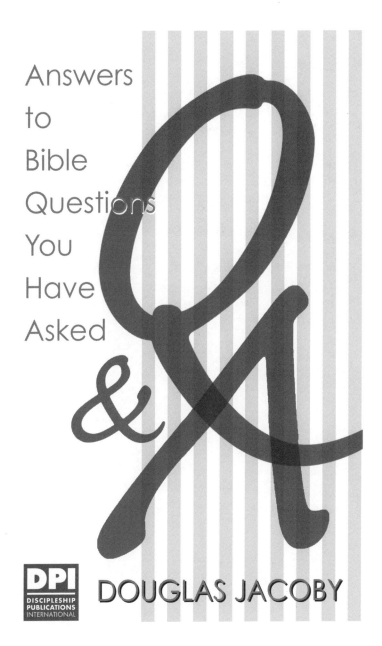

DPI
DISCIPLESHIP
PUBLICATIONS
INTERNATIONAL

DOUGLAS JACOBY

Q & A

© 2001 by Discipleship Publications International
2 Sterling Rd., Billerica, MA 01862-2595

Printed in the United States of America

ISBN: 1-57782-146-7

Cover and Interior Design: Christine Nolan

To Jim Blough—

Wise mentor, upward call
and treasured friend.

Contents

1. Hate Your Family?
2. Saved or Not?
3. What Happens When We Die?
4. The "Fruit" of John 15
5. Are Children Who Die Automatically Saved?
6. Sins Leading to Death
7. Unwholesome Talk
8. Eternal Sin
9. Bible Complete
10. Everyone Saved?
11. Disfellowship
12. "Falling Away"
13. "Restoration"
14. Those Who Haven't Heard
15. Baptism and Awareness of Sin
16. Judges 20

Section 2

1. Veiling
2. Three Days Foretold
3. Least in the Kingdom
4. Levels of Reward
5. Nathanael and the Tree
6. Psalm 137 Too Harsh?
7. The Spirits in Prison
8. God Hardens Hearts?
9. Chapter 24 of *The Spirit*
10. Baptism for the Dead
11. An Evil Spirit from God?
12. The Abomination That Causes Desolation
13. 1 Corinthians 7:14
14. Counterfeit Miracles

Section 3

Section 4

Section 5

Acknowledgments

Credit for this book must go to my friend Mike Taliaferro, who in 1998 urged me to commit to an online column. He foresaw that regular online installments could be transformed into a book. And so, through the groundbreaking work carried out in Johannesburg on the electronic side of Mike's ministry (www.Acesonline.org), the *Q & A* book began to take shape.

In addition, hearty thanks are due to the DPI staff, who deftly re-formed material of miscellaneous types into an organized and structured book. Our working relationship through the years has been a true partnership.

My prayer is that you will benefit as much from this book as many have from the online column. And thanks again, Mike.

Publisher's Note

The majority of the questions answered in this book were originally answered in the author's column, *The Bible on Trial*, which has appeared on the Aces Online Web site. From time to time in this book, the author will reference additional material that can be found in the archives for this column. Simply go to www.Acesonline.org, clicking first on "Douglas Jacoby." This will take you to the page for "The Bible on Trial." On this page, click on the "Questions and Answers" tab for the archived material.

The answers to the questions in this book should not be read as the official position of any church body or of this publisher. They represent the opinion of one careful student of the Scriptures who knows that there may be other answers to many of these questions.

Abbreviations

The Bible on Trial	Douglas Jacoby's online column at Aces Online (www.Acesonline.org)
The God Who Dared	Douglas Jacoby, *The God Who Dared: Genesis from Creation to Babel* (Woburn, Mass.: DPI, 1997)
How to Read the Bible for All Its Worth	Gordon D. Fee and Douglas Stuart, *How to Read the Bible for All Its Worth: A Guide to Understanding the Bible* (Grand Rapids: Zondervan, 1993)
Life to the Full	Douglas Jacoby, *Life to the Full: Practical and Powerful Writings of James, Peter, John & Jude* (Woburn, Mass.: DPI, 1995)
NT	"New Testament" as an adjective
OED	Oxford English Dictionary
OT	"Old Testament" as an adjective
Shining Like Stars	Douglas Jacoby, *Shining Like Stars: The Evangelism Handbook for the New Millennium*, revised and expanded (Woburn, Mass.: DPI, 2000)
The Spirit	Douglas Jacoby, *The Spirit: The Work of the Holy Spirit in the Lives of Disciples* (Woburn, Mass.: DPI, 1998)
True and Reasonable	Douglas Jacoby, *True and Reasonable*, revised and expanded (Woburn, Mass.: DPI, 1999)
The Victory of Surrender	Gordon Ferguson, *The Victory of Surrender*, second edition (Woburn, Mass.: DPI, 1999)

Introduction

Ask Questions!

Are you a person who asks a lot of questions? When you hear instructions, do you repeat them to make sure you got them right? When you're lost, do you ask for help? When, in your reading, you come across a word you do not understand, do you look it up? Asking questions is the only way to progress in your learning.

As God's people, we are called not to an unquestioning faith, but to a faith that grapples with issues, asks the tough questions, and even if there is no answer, remains intellectually honest. A church that discourages questions—that proclaims, "Don't ask questions, just believe!" or "We have always done it that way; why do you have to question it?"—is not a truly Biblical church. If the *Bible* is the authority, then the church is *not*. Receiving the message as the word of God rather than as the word of man (1 Thessalonians 2:13) means any question is in fair territory.

In fact, the only way to read the Bible without having any questions is to read it unthinkingly. The attentive reader will soon find that Bible study is more than simply "reading and obeying" without the middle step of "interpretation." Anyone who says, "You don't need to interpret the Bible; just obey it," is misleading you. While it is true that the basic truths of the Bible are plain for all to see, everything else—most of the Scriptures, in fact—requires disciplined study in order to be understood. Interpretation is merely coming to understand the meaning of a passage, first in its original context and then for today.

'Interpretation'—A Dirty Word?

"Interpretation" is *not* a dirty word. And yet, our natural tendency is to take the path of least resistance. In our fleshliness, we would like to believe that the Bible "interprets itself" without our having to do any work at all! This is wrong and will lead to much frustration. As the people of God, what approaches are we tempted to take?

- *We read from one translation only.* Yet no translation is perfect. Unless you are working from the Hebrew or the Greek, it is best to compare translations. In English, for example, there are many good translations available. Although currently the bestseller is the New International Version (NIV), it is not the "authorized" version any more than the old King James Version is the infallible text. We believe that the original manuscripts were perfect, and yet we must rely first on copies and second on translation. Add to this the cultural distance sometimes between us and a text, and it becomes clear why it is problematic to rely on only one translation.
- *We have poor reading habits.* We read verse-by-verse rather than chapter-by-chapter or (better) book-by-book. The flow of thought is easily lost when we study the scriptures in this way. After all, the chapter numbers were not added till the Middle Ages, and the verse numbers weren't inserted till the midsixteenth century! Breaking apart a section of Scripture and reading it atomistically is not the way to go. If you received a letter in the mail, would you not read it at one sitting? Who would read only a paragraph a day? We must discipline ourselves to follow a train of thought.
- *We "leave passages in the first century,"* as Fee and Stuart[1] put it. When unsure of what a passage means, we tend to say, "Well, this must be 'cultural'; it doesn't apply to us today." Maybe yes, maybe no. But it is dangerous to assume that just because a principle is at odds with our culture or tradition that we are somehow exempt.
- *We treat our leaders like inspired interpreters.* Coming across a troublesome passage, we tend to ask, "What does our church teach on this?" Instead, we should do all we can to determine what the Bible teaches first. After all, maybe the church is wrong! None of us has "arrived"—we all have plenty to learn.
- *We claim, "There's no need to interpret the Bible."* As mentioned above, this is wrong. The Bible never claims that every part is easy to understand (2 Peter 3:14-16), although it urges us to meditate diligently on the Word (Joshua 1:8, Psalm 119:1-176) and apply ourselves (2 Timothy 2:15), in hopes that the Lord will give insight (2 Timothy 2:7).

- *We "spiritualize" the text,* rather than determining what the Holy Spirit originally meant to say. Reading into the text (what Biblical scholars call *eisegesis*) is fanciful and irresponsible. Rather, we should aim to draw out the original meaning of the text (*exegesis*). A common response when this weakness is pointed out is, "As long as the point I'm making is true, it doesn't matter whether this is what my text is saying." What poor methodology! How can you know your point *is* true if your approach to Bible study is so haphazard?

We get into trouble when we follow the crowd in our Bible study habits. I assure you: The hard work will pay off!

Questions Are Good!

Learning can and should be fun. Asking questions is good. It's good when kids ask their parents questions. It's good when students ask their teachers questions. To blithely assume you "got it" the first time through is unrealistic, simplistic, even theologically arrogant.

Some questions are easy, others are hard. (And some are really hard!) So, why try to answer the tough questions? Because they are there and are challenging—like Mt. Everest. And many of the answers we get will help us to complete the picture, appreciate our faith, make our experience richer and enable us to help others who get stuck at some point. Of course we will never answer all the questions. Our salvation and a vital relationship with God do not require that we answer all the questions. As Deuteronomy 29:29 recorded,

> The secret things belong to the LORD our God, but the things revealed belong to us and to our children forever, that we may follow all the words of this law.

We will not necessarily get all the answers we want—now or even in eternity (the Bible never promises omniscience!). And yet, Peter said in 1 Peter 3:15,

> ...Always be prepared to give an answer to everyone who asks you to give the reason for the hope that you have. But do this with gentleness and respect.

He was not just talking about answering doctrinal questions or Bible trivia. He was talking about being able to explain why you have faith in a Jesus who is willing to suffer. The real answers that people need are not usually the ones that focus on the hard passages. Our questions are more than theoretical; there is ultimately a practical motive. We want to be with our God in heaven one day with as many friends as possible.

Getting Answers

We must not leave people with the impression that their faith will be fragile if they cannot answer all the questions. The faith Jesus lauded came from those who probably had almost no answers to the theological sticky wickets, those like the centurion, the Canaanite woman ("even the dogs eat the crumbs") and the poor widow. There is probably no correlation between powerful faith and being able to answer the theological riddles. Being able to answer the tough questions is not to be equated with knowing God. You can be strong in knowledge and logic and still weak in personal faith and surrender. Knowledge can puff up and lead us away from God.

With *Q & A* I would like to think I can tie up all the loose ends, but for some people, the answers given will only raise more questions. You may see some flaws in my logic which seemed flawless to me. My answers may frustrate some of you. You may find that I dismiss an argument because it makes perfect sense for me to do so, but this action may seem quite unsatisfactory to you. Okay, this kind of book may not be for everyone. You will know soon enough if it is helpful to you. If it is not, pass it on. There is probably someone who will be glad you did.

Be a Student and a Teacher

We have much to say about this, but it is hard to explain because you are slow to learn. In fact, though by this time you ought to be teachers, you need someone to teach you the elementary truths of God's word all over again. You need milk, not solid food! Anyone who lives on milk, being still an infant, is not acquainted with the teaching about righteousness. But solid food is for the mature, who

by constant use have trained themselves to distinguish good from evil. (Hebrews 5:11-14)

The Hebrew writer calls his readers to move on from the funda-
mentals into deeper waters. In this passage I see two challenges for
every disciple: being a student and becoming a teacher. The Greek
word for "disciple" is the word "student." Do we have a learning,
inquisitive, teachable spirit? Only when we are true students (true
disciples) can we be spiritual leaders and teachers. So, let me ask
you, are you a diligent student of the Word? And are you teaching
the saved and the lost and being a conduit of God's word into the
lives of others?

Feeding Yourself

Finally, may I offer all readers some general advice on getting
answers to your Bible questions:

- Try to figure out the difficulty or question yourself, using
  whatever Bible tools you have. Aim to teach and train yourself (Hebrews 5:14, Joshua 1:8, 2 Timothy 2:15).
- If you still need help, ask your friends for ideas, leads or
  reading suggestions.
- Speak with the leaders of your ministry; generally speaking,
  the more experienced they are, the better prepared they ought
  to be to assist you with your questions. Let's all call one another higher.
- If you still need help, e-mail a friend outside your local congregation. (Yet this should be as a last resort, not a short-cut
  to personal study.)

How to Use This Book

Q & A is divided into five sections. It is not necessarily a book
you will want to read straight through (though some of you may
find this the easiest way to go).

Section 1	Crucial Issues
Section 2	Difficult Passages
Section 3	Basic Bible
Section 4	Various and Sundry
Section 5	Essays

More Answers Than Questions

At the end of the day, there are more answers than we have questions, for God has the answer to any and every question we could possibly put to him!

Notes

[1] Gordon Fee and Douglas Stuart, *How to Read the Bible for All Its Worth* (Grand Rapids: Zondervan, 1993), 62. This book is highly recommended.

1
Crucial Issues

1. Hate Your Family?

"I was taught that in Luke 14:26 the Greek word for hate means 'love less,' which is what I have taught others. To my surprise, when I looked it up, I saw that it doesn't mean that at all. The Greek word *miseo* means 'to hate, pursue with hatred, detest.' How do you teach this point when explaining discipleship? I want to correctly handle the Word of truth."

This is an excellent question. The sense of what Jesus said is minimized when disciples jump to Matthew 10:37 ("Any-one who loves his father or mother more than me...") for an "explanation" of Luke 14:26. I do not think it is best to explain difficult passages by finding another passage that presents the point in a softer, less pointed form. When I study discipleship with my friends, I turn to Luke 16:13, just a page or so after the "troublesome" 14:26. Here Jesus says that no one can serve two masters; he will, in effect, "love" (serve) one and "hate" the other.

I would encourage you not to use words of Jesus from one section of one gospel to illuminate the meaning of other words of his in another section of an entirely different gospel. Use Luke 16, not Matthew 10, to clarify Luke 14.

2. Saved or Not?

"On the one hand, the Bible urges Christians to be confi-dent that we are saved, and on the other to work out our salvation with 'fear and trembling.' Yet it also seems we are not 'saved' until the Judgment Day. How can a disciple have a soft heart toward these warnings in the Bible, taking them very seriously, and at the same time be confident in his or her salvation?"

Salvation in the Bible is past, present and future. It is past because Jesus died for us before the creation of the world (1 Peter 1). It is present because we receive forgiveness and cleansing on an ongoing basis (1 John 1). And yet it is future because we must *persevere* in order to make it to heaven (Hebrews 3:14). It is all three!

Salvation, on our end of the matter, entails (1) hearing the Word, (2) believing, (3) repenting, (4) being baptized and (5) persevering. Sometimes in our preaching we fail to preach grace, yet at other times we miss the mark in not urging one another to live holy and God-fearing lives (à la Philippians 2:12).

I would also point out that we *are* saved before Judgment Day, and in fact when we die our destiny is sealed, even though Judgment Day may be many years, centuries or even millennia away (in the realm of time). Judgment is not *investigative*—a time when God figures out where we really stand based on our lives, but rather *declarative*—the time at which our guilt or innocence (in Christ) is officially and irrevocably proclaimed. In the meantime, keep your heart soft (Proverbs 4:23)![1]

3. What Happens When We Die?

"I wanted to hear your insight regarding what happens when we die. I've studied the topic some on my own and have gathered that we enter a state of 'rest' or 'sleep' when we die and then are 'awakened' on Judgment Day. I've often heard people say when true Christians die, they are now 'with God,' but it would seem that they are not yet with God. What light can you shed on this topic?"

I believe that when we die, we do not go to heaven or hell, though our reward or punishment begins. The saved are in Paradise, which is a region of Hades. The lost are also in Hades, and their punishment has already begun (2 Peter 2:9). No one goes to heaven or hell before the resurrection (John 5 and many other passages), which does not take place until Jesus returns. At that time we appear before God to be declared innocent through Christ, or guilty. The damned are thrown into the lake of fire; the saved are ushered into heaven.

During the "waiting period" between death and the Judgment Day, we do not sleep. This is simply a common metaphor for death and must be taken figuratively in order not to contradict the Old Testament and New Testament teaching about life after death. We are in "Abraham's bosom"— see Luke 16 (KJV). Yet as awesome as this will be, it is greatly inferior to what awaits us once Jesus returns: a room in the Father's home, a crown of glory, our eternal reward—described in so many different ways in the Bible.

To be frank, this is a position I resisted for nearly twenty years, and yet, from my study of the Scriptures, I see no other way to make sense of all the Biblical evidence. Study it out, and have fun.[2]

4. The 'Fruit' of John 15

"Can you please share your view of fruitfulness in John 15:1-8? I have always been inclined to interpret bearing fruit in this passage as bearing the fruit of the Spirit, the fruit of righteousness, the fruit of good works and the like. The past few years, I have heard a narrow interpretation of John 15—that the 'fruit' is people converted to Christ. A lot of disciples have struggled in their walk with God due to a wrong conclusion drawn from this view. I would appreciate any suggestion as to how I can study John 15 so I can arrive at an understanding of it."

I agree with you. John 15 is broader than winning others to Christ, as essential as that is. It is much more! In the New Testament there are at least six different definitions of the common word "fruit," in addition to the connotation of church growth, as in Colossians 1:6:

1. Literal fruit, such as figs and grapes (Matthew 26:29, Luke 13:7)
2. A relief contribution, as in Romans 15:28
3. Spiritual virtues, as in Ephesians 5:9 and Galatians 5:22-23— and even vices(!), as in Romans 7:5
4. The fruit of repentance, as in Matthew 3:8

5. The effect of someone's life, as in Matthew 7:16
6. Worshipful praise, as in Hebrews 13:15
7. Children in Genesis 17:6-7

Maybe I have even missed a category! In brief, fruit means "productivity" or "leading productive lives," and the specific meaning of fruit must be determined through a careful study of the context of the passage.

I do not want to be misunderstood or misquoted—this is not to say that evangelism is somehow optional. As individuals and as the church, we have been given the commission to lead others to Christ. To reach that goal, we will need to be "bearing fruit" in *every* area specified in the word of God. The more we strive to bear *all* the fruit of which the New Testament speaks, the greater the harvest of "evangelistic fruit" is bound to be. While we all play different roles in the Great Commission (1 Corinthians 3:6ff), we all are under obligation to let our light shine, to articulate the gospel and to love a lost and dying world, just as God in Christ reached out to us. Preach the Word!

5. Are Children Who Die Automatically Saved?

"We know from 1 Peter 2 that all Christians have come into the light from the darkness. At what point does a child enter into darkness? If it is at the point when they first sin, some children at the ages of four or five commit willful sin, yet at that age they are not likely to understand the implications of devoting their lives to Christ. What are the spiritual implications of a child dying after committing knowledgeable sin but before reaching the teen years when they are old enough to make a decision to come to Christ?"

The Bible simply does not say at what precise point a child becomes lost, even though the fact that they do enter that state seems a fair conclusion from our observations of children's behavior and the requirements of the gospel.

Speaking of mankind, Genesis 8:21 says, "every inclination of his heart is evil from childhood." Of course there's a difference between inclination and actual sin or guilt. I actually believe our children commit willful sin long before age five. The real question, though, is how God views them—are they accountable or not?

Yes, the kingdom of heaven belongs to "children," as Jesus put it. A basic Biblical principle is "where the Bible is silent, we cannot be dogmatic." It would be wrong to *insist* that those who never had the ability to "process" the gospel are lost. That would presumably apply to those born retarded and to young children. It's really a moot point because, just as with adults who are "not ready" to listen to the Word, there is only so much we can do. We must help our children to understand God's message at each level of maturity, and the rest we must leave in God's hands. And yet I believe it may be equally wrong to *insist* that all children, when they die, are saved. I tend to think they are, but it is difficult to prove that from the Bible. God's ways are inscrutable; only his revealed will gives us a solid basis for dogma. I suspect that my wife and I will wrestle with this issue as our three children near the age when they make the vital decision to put Jesus first (two of them are now preteens).

On a comforting note, the Bible does seem to say that we will see these "little ones" again. David commented, "But now that [my infant] is dead…can I bring him back again? I will go to him, but he will not return to me" (2 Samuel 12:23). There will be a day when those of us who have lost young children will be reunited with them.

6. Sins Leading to Death

"In 1 John 5:16-17 the author writes that there are some sins that lead to death and others that do not. I have always believed that all sin—any sin—is enough to separate us from God. This passage confuses me."

Thank you for admitting that you are confused about the passage. (Don't worry; you aren't alone!) "A sin that leads to death" is, I believe, singular, not plural. There are not some sins that lead to death and others that are okay. As I understand things (and wrote in *Life to the Full*), the sin leading to death is the sin that one refuses to repent of (Proverbs 28:13). Others, sensitive to the Gnostic background of the false teachers troubling John's churches, say this sin is rejecting Jesus. This would include taking on a heretical position about who Christ is (the heretics were denying that Jesus even had a physical body!).

Yes, all sin leads to death, but that is a *process.* James 1:13-15 does not say that when you give in to temptation you are "dead." That comes about only when sin is "full-grown."

7. Unwholesome Talk

"Ephesians 4:29 says 'Don't let any unwholesome talk come out of your mouths....' Is the use of slang words like 'gosh' and 'gee' unwholesome, or is it profanity (Exodus 20:7)? Brother, please help me understand these issues so that I can help myself and other disciples around me—especially with the second question, because many disciples, including me, use these words."

I do appreciate your question, and I share your concern about unwholesome talk. I distinguish between profanity and coarseness. Profanity is always wrong; coarseness may be more relatively defined, depending on who you are with at the time. I will not repeat profane words. My wife and I will not even allow our children to use coarse language, though the latter is very common in the world and even in the church.

There are many, many phrases in English that I think are vulgar ("I don't give a ____," "Shoot," etc.). They are often transparent circumlocutions or euphemisms for worldly, profane speech. Eventually, in the evolution of a language, once coarse or even profane phrases may "lose" their original sense and even become acceptable dictionary entries. (Not that we look to the world for what we may and may not say, of course!) One example of this is the names of the days of the week, which were named after pagan deities: the sun god, the moon god, Ty, Woden, Thor, Frigg and Saturn.

Yet the phrases I would like to comment on are some things we say that have definite religious connotations. None of these words is "profane" in the common sense of that word. Included are the two words you specifically asked about. Where I have not been sure, I have consulted the OED.

I realize that for many people, the religious connotation of these words has all but been lost. And yet to many ears, these words are reminiscent of their original forms. I remember my grandmother correcting me when I said "Gee." I truly did not understand what was wrong with that, though I changed my speech. That may have been in the '60s, and yes, the times, they are a-changing, but we are responsible for every careless word that comes out of our mouths (Matthew 12:36). Even today I would hesitate to use any of the following expressions:

- Gosh, Golly—from "God"
- Gee—probably from "Jesus"
- Darn, Dang—from "damn"
- What the ___? —from "hell"
- Holy ___. —implies "God," one of the "saints," etc.
- Egad(s)—from "ye God(s)" (a hangover from paganism)
- Heavens, Heavens to ___. —mentions "heaven"
- Jesus, Bejesus—a clear taking of the Lord's name in vain
- Christ, Jesus Christ, God—a clear taking of the Lord's name in vain
- For God's/Christ's/Jesus' sake—nearly always a taking of the Lord's name in vain
- Ever-living—refers to God, "who alone is immortal"

I hope this is helpful. I think we are in the realm of opinion matters (Romans 14-15) when we draw up lists of words to be avoided. "Each one should be fully convinced in his own mind" (14:5). In the meantime, bear with those who take a different view. Keep yourself righteous, but not self-righteous. And remember, there may be children listening!

8. Eternal Sin

"In Mark 3:29 Jesus speaks about an eternal sin for which no one will be forgiven. It states that whoever blasphemes against the Holy Spirit will be condemned. Is the word 'blasphemes' written in the present tense—i.e. a person who continues to blaspheme and, not repenting, will never be forgiven—or does it refer to anyone who has ever blasphemed against the Holy Spirit?"

Excellent question, and one to which we will shortly return. And yet, to begin with, I would like to make a comment to all our readers, and especially to those who are even a little bit familiar with ancient Greek.

I personally would not make too much of a particular tense in the Greek. In Koine Greek, the present is usually a progressive, just as the aorist indicates a specific time, but this is not always the case. The New Testament is full of contrary examples! Bottom line, Greek grammatical issues are not usually resolved without a good, working knowledge of Greek—obtainable with a minimum of three years of language study at the university level. We need to resist the temptation to dabble in Greek, as though a mere knowledge of the alphabet or possession of an interlinear somehow qualifies us to reason on the level of experts who have devoted their lives to the study of this beautiful language.

To your question: Since Paul says he was a blasphemer (1 Timothy 1)—directly as well as one who attempted to force others to blaspheme—he is as good a candidate as any for one who may have committed "the eternal sin." And yet the Lord forgave Paul! I believe this shows us that regardless of what we have done in our pasts, there can be forgiveness and genuine hope for change. (See also 1 Corinthians 6:9-11.)

It is also important to consider the context of the passage. In Mark 3 religious leaders, who had seen the evidence of Jesus' identity and authority with their own eyes, still refused to believe. This demonstrates a hardness of heart (as in Proverbs 29:1), from which there was no recovery. And yet, you may ask, was not Paul in a similar condition when he, as Pharisee and church persecutor, strove with all his might to oppose the church? Apparently he had not "crossed the line"—he had not hardened himself irretrievably. We should resist the urge to "play God," assessing who has and who has not committed "the eternal sin."

Finally, it is an "eternal" sin because of its consequences in the next age. In Greek (as well as in Latin) the words "age" and "eternal" are related as noun and adjective. "Eternal" carries the sense not so much of infinity as of the world to come, for we cannot reject and refuse God in this life and expect to share in eternal life in the world to come.

9. Bible Complete

"How can I be sure that today's Bible is complete?"

The short response to your question:[3]

1. The New Testament expresses the assurance that the Old Testament is inspired.
2. The inspiration of the New Testament is guaranteed by its apostolic connection to Jesus Christ.
3. Other writings, penned much later than the apostolic period and contradicting the Scriptures, were unable to win acceptance in the canon.

10. Everyone Saved?

"My question is regarding how disciples should respond to people (relatives) when they say that Jesus died for everyone's sins (past, present and future), and therefore they are saved. This kind of comment totally disregards repentance and makes it seem like everyone is saved without any effort. What I am looking for is a straightforward answer that does not take much preaching, especially since this situation involves a relative (a parent)."

I would use verses that, without too much interpretation, "lay it out," making it obvious that there is more to salvation than the fact that Jesus died on the cross for us. Consider the following passages, chosen among the hundreds of potentially useful to refute the "broad road" view of Jesus and his teachings:

1. "…without holiness no one will see the Lord" (Hebrews 12:14)
2. "…source of eternal salvation for all who obey him" (Hebrews 5:9)
3. "Make every effort…." (Luke 13:24)

11. Disfellowship

"What are the criteria for disfellowship?—1 Corinthians 5:11 seems to indicate specific sins (of which the believer will not repent), coupled with calling oneself a 'brother' as the only criteria. Is there any other scripture that may indicate otherwise?"

Disfellowshipping is a very serious matter, warranted by grave sin (unrepented of) or false teaching (actively trying to turn others from the church), as in Titus 3. The local eldership makes the call, issuing the notice with love and with sensitivity to any legal implications. I believe the words about calling oneself a brother are meant primarily to distinguish between a church member and an outsider. (We don't disfellowship nonmembers.)

12. 'Falling Away'

"I talked to a brother today who fell away some time ago but came back several years ago. He is having difficulty with Hebrews 6:4-6, for he thinks it says that once someone has fallen away, they had their shot. He thinks that even though he is 'back,' he will probably not be forgiven in the end. He cites the Israelites and Esau as examples. I know that that is a difficult passage, and early church writers differ on its interpretation. What do you think about this passage?"

The Bible seems to distinguish between those who have "wandered away" (James 5:19) and those who have "fallen away" (Hebrews 6:4). For those in the first category there is hope; for those in the second, none. In light of Hebrews 6, perhaps it would be clearer to state that if they have been brought back, they had not actually crossed the point of no return (Hebrews 6:4, Proverbs 29:1).

Incidentally, when Jesus predicts that his apostles will, on the night of his arrest, "all fall away," this is a different verb from what is normally used for "falling" or "falling away." (To illustrate, the verb in connection with these predictions is consistently translated "be offended" in the King James Version.) Hence, we must distinguish between stumbling and falling. It is very possible that the terminology about "falling away" which has become so common among us should be revisited.

13. 'Restoration'

[continued from question 12] "Yet we practice 'restoration.' What exactly is Hebrews 6 referring to? What about James 5:19-20, that if one wanders away from the truth, we should bring him back?"

"Restoration" has become a technical term for persuading someone who has left the fold to return. In the Bible the term appears several times, though not necessarily with the same meaning. Let's consider two well-known passages:

> The Lord is my shepherd, I shall not be in want.
>   He makes me lie down in green pastures,
> he leads me beside quiet waters,
>   he restores my soul.
> He guides me in paths of righteousness
>   for his name's sake. (Psalm 23:1-3)

> Brothers, if someone is caught in a sin, you who
> are spiritual should restore him gently. But watch
> yourself, or you also may be tempted. Carry each
> other's burdens, and in this way you will fulfill the
> law of Christ. (Galatians 6:1-2)

As we see in Psalm 23, we all need restoring from time to time, don't we? And in Galatians 6 we see that restoration involves helping out a brother or sister who has become stuck, having lost perspective (and perhaps with it the faith, hope and drive to see recovery).

I would suggest that we speak of "bringing someone back," that is, bringing back someone who has drifted away, because restoration (a sort of "spiritual recovery") is usually something we do to those who have not left the fold.

14. Those Who Haven't Heard

"What happens to those people who have not heard the gospel yet, if Jesus were to come today? Would they have a chance to come to repentance?"

According to John 3:18, those who do not believe are in trouble. If it were possible for those ignorant of the Word to be saved, then evangelism wouldn't be essential, would it? In fact, we might mess up someone's chances to make it by making mistakes in how we present the gospel. And yet Jesus, who knew we would do a less than perfect job, commanded us to make disciples of all nations. No one will be saved by being a decent person, for *all* have fallen short (Romans 3:23). Thus it is imperative that we get the Word out! People are not lost because they have not heard the gospel. They are lost because they are in sin.

15. Baptism and Awareness of Sin

"According to Acts 2, to become a Christian we must repent and be baptized. Exactly what is "repentance" referring to? In Acts it does not appear that an in-depth knowledge of everything that is sin was required for salvation. What do you think? How much understanding of sin is required for a valid baptism?"

I think you are probably right. Our understanding of sin and appreciation of our lostness apart from God increases not just during the time we are studying the Bible to become followers of Jesus, but afterward as well. When we say, "Jesus is Lord," we mean it to the best of our knowledge and ability at the time. Certainly, our walk with God deepens as time goes by. For example, we would not expect a newly licensed driver to drive with the wisdom or experience that comes only with years of practice. Ephesians 4:21-24 describes the process of repentance as we come to know Christ, while Ephesians 4:25-32 demands that we *continue* to change.

16. Judges 20

"Why in Judges 20 do we see Israel going to battle for a righteous cause (punishing the Benjamites for the rape and murder of the concubine), being encouraged by God to do so, and yet losing twice and losing many soldiers in the process? Was God testing their resolve in dealing with the Benjamite sin? Or is there some other reason?"

How true to life the passage rings! We mean to do well. We try and try again, yet we too fall to the ground. And it can be so discouraging. The Bible does not say whether God was testing their resolve; we can only guess the deeper issues in play. When we read the narrative passages of the Bible, such as Judges 17-21, we need to take special care not to look for morals when the Word itself does not make them clear. The main point of the end of Judges is that without a king, things were very bad indeed. When everyone does right in his own eyes (21:25), atrocious things happen. Righting the situation is seldom as easy as "one, two, three." God may be with us, but this does not mean that we will not have to go through many hardships to enter the kingdom of God.

Notes

[1] For more on this subject, you may enjoy my exposition of 1 John in *Life to the Full.*

[2] For more information on this topic see the appendix in my book *The God Who Dared*, which is entitled "Another Day in Paradise: What Happens When We Die?" See also question 11a in the Aces Online archives.

[3] If you want a more complete answer, refer to the archived material in *The Bible on Trial* on Aces Online. There are thirty-four units, which you should find useful. In addition, you will find recommendations for further reading.

2
Difficult Passages

1. Veiling

"I am concerned with the question of veiling. Why are Christian sisters today not veiled per 1 Corinthians 11:6?"

The veil is not an issue to most Christians today who interpret the admonishment to practice veiling as culturally specific, like footwashing and the holy kiss. In Paul's day, respectable women throughout the Mediterranean world wore the veil, pagans and Christians alike. Today, interestingly, in many Muslim countries women are veiled, and in many parts of the world, a kiss is not an uncommon form of greeting (man to man, woman to woman, that is).

One reason I believe this to be a cultural issue is that there is no mention of a veil in the Biblical account of God making clothing for Adam and Eve *after* the Fall. (The clothes were of animal skins—can you imagine a full-length animal skin veil?!)

Another reason is that even today, we can clearly observe the effect on our mission of the exact same convention. Consider that in some parts of the world (say, in the more radical Islamic states) the veil is *still* required in public. In those places, its absence would seriously hinder the gospel, while in most other places, the effect would be the exact *opposite:* If the veil were worn, the gospel would be needlessly discredited—1 Corinthians 9 shows the wisdom of becoming all things to all men (and women).

This passage does refer to principles that are laid out fully elsewhere in the Bible, namely, that women are to be modest and that wives are to respect their husbands. An equivalent present-day negative example would be a Christian woman wearing a plunging neckline in public or criticizing her husband in front of others, demonstrating a lack of modesty and undermining her husband's God-ordained leadership.

The issue of culture and interpretation is important and deserves much more explanation than I am prepared to offer at this time. Christians may honestly disagree over the meaning of 1 Corinthians 11, yet no matter how one interprets the passage, this issue is not central to salvation, but is rather a peripheral doctrinal matter.

I agree completely that veiling is a cultural issue, and that this answers the most superficial question of how disciples of Jesus are to apply this passage today. And I acknowledge that without dissecting the passage, we may well be missing deeper theological truths that the Spirit wants us to understand.

2. Three Days Foretold

"In Luke 24:46 Jesus tells the disciples that it is written that 'the Christ will suffer and rise from the dead on the third day.' The only OT scripture I can find that comes close to saying this is Hosea 6:2. Can you explain to me what Jesus meant?"

Yes, I would guess that passages like Hosea 6:2 and Jonah 1:17 are what Jesus had in mind. As you detect, this is not exactly "prophecy" in the usual sense, but rather foreshadowing. Often the Old Testament foreshadows the New Testament messianic events. One fabulous example of foreshadowing is the "sacrifice" of Isaac in Genesis 22, which parallels the sacrifice of Christ in numerous ways. In addition, the messianic Psalm 16 (see article 33 in *The Bible on Trial*) indicates that the Christ would soon rise from the dead.

3. Least in the Kingdom

"Would you please explain what Jesus meant in Luke 7:28? Jesus says, 'I tell you, among those born of women there is no one greater than John; yet the one who is least in the kingdom of God is greater than he.' What was John's greatness? Is Jesus the 'least in the kingdom of God'? Should we seek a greatness different from John the Baptist's?"

"Greater" refers not to a spirit of passion or heroism, nor to his accomplishments, for who will accomplish what John did in his lifetime? I believe the "greater" pertains to position. John, in one sense, was not *in* the kingdom, whereas followers of Jesus *are* in the kingdom (Colossians 1:12-13). Those who lived and died under the old covenant (Jewish Law), like John, experienced their relationship with God less directly than we do (Ephesians 2:18). They would be made complete only with us, the Bible says (Hebrews 11:40). Most important, under that covenant the indwelling Spirit was not given to believers—this happened only after Jesus' ascension (John 7:39-40). As a result, we enjoy a great position and a greater intimacy with God in our spirituality. And this is something to thank God for!

4. Levels of Reward

"You mentioned that there are varying degrees of punishment regarding nondisciples, which I think is true (Luke 12:47-48), but you then used Matthew 6:20 and Philippians 4:17 to argue in favor of degrees of reward for disciples as well. I was wondering how this is reconcilable with the 'complete' salvation that Christ gives to every disciple. I always tended to think that just as 'more grace' doesn't make us 'more saved,' so 'more treasures' doesn't mean 'more reward.' Levels of reward also seem to me to nullify the idea of our service being only a response to our salvation—instead, our service begins to be a measure of our reward."

Eight years ago, when I first wrote my paper about heaven and hell, I advanced the idea that the experience of heaven and hell will depend on the individual's life—his choices, opportunities, thoughts, words, deeds. In Luke 12 some are beaten with few blows, some with many. To tell the truth, I continued to resist the notion of "treasure in heaven" because I felt it might encourage wrong motives. I thought the Reformation sorted out the Catholic error and saw no need to go back there! Eventually I changed my mind because I came to the conviction that this is what the Bible teaches.

Yet I frankly do not see how degrees of reward or treasure in heaven in any way nullifies grace or salvation. Who taught "complete salvation" more than the apostle Paul? And yet what do we do with Colossians 1:24? Doesn't the Bible in many passages teach we will be judged according to what we have done, not only according to what Christ has done for us? Isn't it *both*? Philippians 2:12, James 2:20-24 and other verses give me the idea that service is *not merely* a *response* to salvation—though I teach it and it feels right. It is a response, but it's also an identification with Christ (Philippians 3:10-11).

So I would say, to amplify the common analogy about Judgment Day, that the "exam" may not be pass/fail. Perhaps letter grades will be given as well! Yet I have never met a disciple who seemed controlled by this consideration. It may be there in the back of our minds, but the pressures of life, the refining fires of personal sacrifice and the opposition of the world continually purge us from being sinfully motivated by our reward.

I hope I am right about all this, because, as I think you know, we who teach (which applies to all disciples to some extent) will be judged "more strictly" (James 3:1).

5. Nathanael and the Tree

"How do you interpret John 1:48? My wife and I got a chance to see a fig tree in the Atlanta Botanical Gardens once. It is an interesting tree in that its leaves are large, and they extend all the way to the bottom of the tree, such that it would be fairly easy to hide near its trunk. Is that the idea in this passage? Was Nathanael praying under a fig tree, where no one (but God) could see him?"

I have never come across the hiding motif in any commentator, though I may have missed something. Whatever Nathanael was doing under the tree—and God isn't telling us!—Jesus knew. Our focus is on Nathanael's response of faith, not the nature of his activity under the tree. Personally, I love the way Jesus sees the good in this honest Israelite. He tells him in verse 51 that he will see the angels "ascending and descending" on the Son of Man. This is a reference to Genesis 28:12—Jacob's ladder. Angels entered the presence of God by way of this ladder. John 1:48 anticipates

John 14:6. Thus, for us Jesus is the "Stairway to Heaven." What a thought! Nathanael will come to appreciate Jesus as far more than a clairvoyant or prophet; he will in time come to appreciate him as the only way to God.

6. Psalm 137 Too Harsh?

"Isn't Psalm 137:9 a little harsh? This is the only verse in the Bible that in my view does not seem to describe God's heart as I have known it. But, being in the Bible, I want to know how to read it."

I appreciate your asking this question and your honesty about how it makes you feel. I agree with you—this passage does not describe God's heart, neither as you have known it nor as I have. Does this sound unorthodox? It may help to remember that the Psalms constitute a sort of prayer book, faithfully reflecting the outpourings of heart of the men of God some 2500 or 3000 years ago. God allowed this troubling verse to remain in the Psalter, but why? Perhaps it is left to be an encouragement to us also to pour out our hearts, to share our true feelings, rather than going through the motions and praying or saying the "right" things. Honesty is commendable—the honesty of this psalmist (living out the Babylonian exile and bitterly struggling with his faith) and yours as well! Know this: Even though "shocking" things may be prayed, the Lord listens, discerns our true heart and does not "shoot us down" when we are open with him. Candor needs to join faith and persistence if we are to pray as genuinely as the psalmist.

7. The Spirits in Prison

"I would like to find out the explanation to the scripture in Peter where it mentions Jesus, after he was crucified, 'preaching to the spirits in prison.' We understand that he was buried for three days, but where was he during those three days? Does it mean that he actually was in hell, or are there many different explanations as to where he might have been?"

Yes, there are a number of ideas about where Jesus was and what he did during that Easter weekend of 30 AD. One common understanding is that during this period Jesus descended into the realm of the dead and declared the gospel message. The "Apostles' Creed" affirms this, though the phrase in the creed "descended into hell" refers not to any postcrucifixion punishment falling on Jesus. Rather, "hell" is an older English word for the abode of the dead; its meaning has changed now to a place of punishment.

According to the Scriptures, Jesus did not ascend to heaven (from Bethany, on the back slope of the Mount of Olives) until forty days after his resurrection (John 20:17; Luke 24:50; Acts 1:3, 12). So maybe it was during this interval that Jesus spoke to the dead, if we are interpreting 1 Peter 3:19 and 4:6 correctly.

The exact nature of this "preaching" continues to be a matter of debate among scholars. As a matter of fact, I myself have begun to change my own previously published interpretation of this very intriguing passage![1]

8. God Hardens Hearts?

"How are we to understand God's hardening of Pharaoh's heart?"

I believe that when you go back to Exodus you will see that in some passages it says that God hardened his heart, while in others it says that Pharaoh hardened his own heart—and in others both aspects are described. My opinion is that these hardenings are one and the same or are occurring at the same time.

To illustrate, it has been said that the sun melts ice and hardens clay. Two factors determine the outcome: the action or energy applied to the substance and the substance itself. The ice does not melt and the clay harden because the sun favors one over the other; rather, each responds to the heat according to its own nature. In this passage God applied the pressure, and Pharaoh responded. Since Pharaoh, unlike ice and clay, has free will in responding to God, he is ultimately accountable for his response. In other words, God is fair, and his laws apply fairly and equally to all.

9. Chapter 24 of The Spirit

"I have some questions about chapter 24 of your book *The Spirit*:

> (a) Is 'they' in Acts 2:1 referring to the twelve apostles or the 120?
>
> (b) Does the prophecy Joel spoke of mean preaching or an infallible doctrinal gift?
>
> (c) Was Paul's apostleship a special version? How did he get it?
>
> (d) You said on page 212 that Ananias laid his hands on Paul so that he would receive his sight, but Acts 9:17 also says 'and be filled with the Holy Spirit.' How is this explained?
>
> (e) In Acts 15:9, in referring to Cornelius, Peter said that God 'purified their hearts by faith.' No one has ever used this scripture with me to justify forgiveness of sins before baptism, but I cannot see why they could not. Besides using the obvious scriptures about baptism, how would you explain this verse?"

First of all, I appreciate your taking the time to read the entire book, and I am happy to try to clarify the matters you wrote about. As for (a), I believe the group refers to the apostles. All are Galileans, after all, according to the text. Jesus had a sizable contingent up in Galilee (five hundred or more), as well as his group in the south, the 120. I realize that some of the 120 may also have been in the 500. Anyway, the men of Galilee are almost certainly the apostles.

As for the nature of the prophecy Joel spoke of (Joel 2:28-32), my answer to question (b) is *neither*. Certainly it seems to have been more than preaching, and yet to claim that those who received the prophetic gift were infallible or on an equal level with the apostles seems unwarranted. After all, John 14:26 and 16:13 are promises for the apostles, not for any other leaders.

Paul (c) claimed to receive his apostleship specially (Galatians 1:11-12), and it was indeed a "special version," to the point that he describes himself in 1 Corinthians 15 as "one abnormally born."

As for (d), Paul was not filled with the Spirit until he received the Spirit in baptism. Remember, people can be healed with or without being Christians. Contrary to the claims of the neo-Pentecostals, the state of one's heart is not a condition for his or her being healed. As you study this further, you may want to read over chapters 16-18 again. (Don't forget the footnotes, which contain most of the more advanced information.)

Finally (e), Acts 10:43 does not say they were saved at that point. Faith may purify your heart, but that doesn't mean you are saved. Besides, Peter said in Acts 11:16 that at this point in his message (the divine interruption) he had only begun to speak; he hadn't delivered the whole message necessary for salvation. This is why, after the miracle from God, he continues (or accelerates) his talk and tells them *how* to have their sins forgiven through Jesus' name (10:48).

The following diagram might be helpful. It summarizes the responses necessary for salvation.

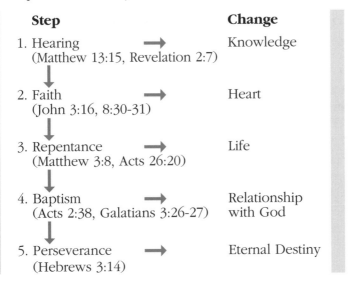

Step		Change
1. Hearing	→	Knowledge
(Matthew 13:15, Revelation 2:7)		
2. Faith	→	Heart
(John 3:16, 8:30-31)		
3. Repentance	→	Life
(Matthew 3:8, Acts 26:20)		
4. Baptism	→	Relationship with God
(Acts 2:38, Galatians 3:26-27)		
5. Perseverance	→	Eternal Destiny
(Hebrews 3:14)		

The practice of "accepting Christ" or "praying Jesus into your heart" is one of today's most common evangelical experiences, despite the fact that it flouts scriptural requirements for salvation. An invention of American religious revivalists of the early 1800s, this heretical doctrine is based on misinterpretation of narrowly selected scriptures. It is easily refuted:

- Revelation 3:20, written to lukewarm Christians, does not support it.
- John 1:12 does not support it.
- There is an inadequate focus on discipleship (Colossians 2:6-7).
- Receiving Christ (John 12:47-48) means accepting him on his terms, not inviting him into your heart.

10. Baptism for the Dead

"What was Paul referring to about the baptism for the dead? What are your thoughts, and what do you know about it?"

Surely 1 Corinthians 15:29 is one of the most problematic passages in the entire Bible! There are four or five main interpretations, and I will not go into them all at this time. I would suggest you consult any commentary on 1 Corinthians, and you will find them. Counting all the alternatives, I have read a couple of articles that listed some forty different interpretations! (Better not be too dogmatic here, brothers!) The one interpretation that is impossible is the Mormon view that you can be baptized for one of your ancestors. Colossians 2:12 and other passages teach that it is only your own faith when you are baptized that will enable you to be saved. Keep in mind that 1 Corinthians 15 is a chapter on the resurrection (which some teachers in Corinth were questioning) and that whatever view we come to, it needs to fit within the flow of Paul's thought. If there is no resurrection of the body, the dead will never make it to heaven. (See my comments in *The Bible on Trial*, question 11b.) Paul insists that we are ultimately in a hopeless condition if we are not going to be raised from the dead.

11. An Evil Spirit from God?

"In 1 Samuel 16:14 and 19:9 it states that an evil spirit from the Lord came upon Saul, and in James 1:13 it states that God does not tempt anyone. How is it that God is able to send an evil spirit?"

The short answer: In the Bible, particularly in the Old Testament, secondary causes are often described as though they were primary causes. Since everything that happens God either (1) wills *directly* (causes) or (2) wills *indirectly* (allows to take place), it is true that nothing happens apart from the will of God.

The ancient Hebrews often describe events of the second category as though they belonged to the first. In this way, everything is attributed to God. The trick is to figure out whether something is being merely allowed (as presumably in 1 Samuel 19, a chapter in which a "good" spirit also is dispatched from God later on in verses 21-23). So in the verses you cite, God sends evil spirits (indirect causality). There is no compromise of God's purity, since this spirit does not flow from God (directly).

As for the tempting, Satan of course is the tempter (Matthew 4:3); God merely uses the work of Satan (indirectly) to *test* us.

I know this way of describing secondary causes probably feels strange, but one simply must accept this way of talking about events. It is very common in the Bible. (See for example Isaiah 45:7.)

12. The Abomination That Causes Desolation

"What exactly is the abomination that causes desolation?"

I believe you are referring to Jesus' prophecy in Matthew 24:15 (Mark 13:14), which is a reference back to the book of Daniel. Whether the abomination (Daniel 9:27) was originally a pagan image set up in the Holy of Holies (Most Holy Place, NIV) or the sacrificing of swine flesh on the altar of the temple, it was something idolatrous that desecrated the temple (Hosea 9:10). For the historical background, see the apocryphal books of 1-2 Maccabees, which describe the bravery of the Jews who resisted pagan influence in the second century BC.

Jesus in the "mini-apocalypse" of Matthew 24 (and its parallels) is prophesying the desecration of the temple in 70 AD at the hands of the Romans, which would parallel the similar desecration which took place two and a half centuries earlier at the hands of the Antiochus Epiphanes IV (Daniel 11:31). So, the abomination has to do with the abominable desecration of the temple at the hands of pagans. While the destruction of the temple does not mean a lot to us today, it was highly significant in the first century when Jesus predicted the end of the Jewish sacrificial system.

His stunned disciples could scarcely fathom that the temple, in all its glory, could be slated for destruction. But Jesus warned them that this omen would signal that it was time to flee. History records that those who accepted Jesus' words did just that. They fled to the town of Pella and were able to avoid the imbroglio of the First Jewish War (66-73 AD).

For further study, take a peek at:

- John Oakes' new book, *Daniel: Prophet to the Nations* (Highlands Ranch, Colorado: Great Commission Illustrated, 2000).
- Jim McGuiggan's *The Book of Daniel* (Fort Worth: Star Bible Publications, 1978).
- Joyce G. Baldwin's *Daniel (Tyndale series)* (Downers Grove: Intervarsity, 1978).
- C. F. Keil and F. Delitzsch, *Ezekiel and Daniel* (Nashville: Hendrickson, 1996). This is a translation and reprint from the German original of 1866-91.

13. 1 Corinthians 7:14

"In 1 Corinthians 7:14, what does the word 'sanctified' mean? Does it mean 'saved'? Can an unbelieving spouse be saved through the believing spouse?"

I believe Paul is simply urging a believing spouse not to hasten separation from an unbelieving one too quickly because this compromises the unbeliever's chances of becoming a Christian. Whether the "sanctification" implies potential salvation, special setting apart unto the plan of God must be determined from the context of 1 Corinthians. To answer your question directly, "Yes, an unbelieving spouse *can* be saved through the believing spouse." "Yes"—assuming that the believing spouse is patient and does not break off the relationship. He/she can be saved—but he/she isn't saved *yet*.

14. Counterfeit Miracles

"I have a fellow on the ship who is a charismatic. He has real-life experiences with miracles, including one instance with his wife. She had developed bumps of some sort on her back and after their minister prayed over her, they were gone. My heart tells me he isn't lying, but after seeking advice and asking questions, I still am not satisfied. I've been told that the devil masquerades as an angel of light, yet my interpretation of the Bible is that no one can perform miracles unless God is with him. If you have some wisdom on this, I would appreciate another perspective."

While it is rarely productive to challenge someone else's "miraculous" experiences, it is important to evaluate them from a scriptural perspective. The Bible does say that Satan is into *counterfeit* miracles. They are not necessarily genuine; they only imitate or approximate the real thing. (See 2 Thessalonians 2:9-11, for example.) And yet the Bible records that sometimes those who do not know God perform amazing feats. Please read Acts 19 (the seven sons of Sceva, Jews who truly exorcised demons) and Deuteronomy 13 (an even more amazing passage). See also chapter 16, especially pages 129-130, of *The Spirit,* a book I wrote specifically to address these sorts of questions.

15. Led into Temptation?

In Matthew 6:13, Jesus prays that God 'lead us not into temptation, but deliver us from the evil one.' Why would he pray this, if God cannot tempt us?"

God tempts no one, according to James 1:13. If "tempt" in Matthew 6 is the same word and meaning as "tempt" in James 1, there would seem to be a contradiction. Yet as you know, the same word can be used in different ways in different passages and contexts. There are at least two meanings of "tempt":

- Test—with the connotation of proving, refining or strengthening (Matthew 6).
- Entice—with the aim of breaking down one's resistance so that the person will give in to sin (James 1).

In the Lord's Prayer, it is the first sense of the word that Jesus is using. Not that we are never to be tested in this sense! The prayer is that we will not be led into temptation that would overwhelm us. God's solid promise of 1 Corinthians 10:13 stands! He will not test us with greater pressure than we are able to endure.

Another approach views Matthew 6 as simply a prayer saying, "help us stay away from temptation," "don't let us get entangled in it." I would compare this prayer to one like we find in Psalm 7:6.

> Arise, O Lord, in your anger;
> rise up against the rage of my enemies.
> Awake, my God; decree justice.

We don't need to tell God to arise or to awake. He will do both of those just fine without us. In the same way, we don't need to tell him to not lead us into temptation (since he has no intention of doing that), but such prayers express our need for God in dramatic ways. Both the prayer in Psalm 7 and the prayer in Matthew 6 can be seen as expressions of our need and affirmations of God's ability to deliver us. Given this approach, the temptations of Matthew 6 and James 1 are the same and God will not lead us into them.

16. Mark 9:38-41 and Luke 11:23

"In Mark 9:38-41, there is a situation in which the disciples tell a man who is not one of Jesus' followers to stop driving out demons in his name, and Jesus tells them, 'Do not stop him. No one who does a miracle in my name can in the next moment say anything bad about me, for whoever is not against us is for us.' Then in Luke 11:23, Jesus teaches that, 'He who is not with me is against me, and he who does not gather with me, scatters.' How do these two situations harmonize?"

The confusion is fairly easily dispelled when you look at who Jesus was talking to. With the man in Mark 9 we are dealing with an earnest follower who was not "one of us" as the apostles saw it, yet was sincere about his faith in Jesus. The apostles wanted to exclude him on sectarian grounds, but Jesus saw his heart and rebuked their exclusiveness. In Luke 11 Jesus is speaking to those who are accusing him of being in league with Beelzebub. He makes it clear that those who have not aligned themselves with him are certainly against him, perhaps to say to all bystanders that they have a clear choice and they cannot stay neutral in such a conflict. Two such different circumstances result in two different pronouncements from Jesus.

One way to harmonize the passage is by understanding Jesus to be saying, in effect, that the man in Mark 9 is in fact with Jesus and gathering with him. What do you think about that possibility?

Bottom line, Jesus insists that we make a choice. These two passages indicate clearly that there is no neutrality: when it comes to our commitment, there are only two possibilities. That is how I think the passages mesh together.

17. The Three Days

"According to Matthew 12:40, 'the Son of Man will be three days and three nights in the heart of the earth' (NIV). Now if Jesus was crucified on Friday (the day before the Sabbath—John 19:31) and rose on Sunday morning (Luke 24:1-3), that leaves only Friday night and Saturday night that he was 'in the...earth.' This is only two nights. I can live with part of Friday, all of Saturday and part of Sunday being the 'three days,' but what of the 'three nights' noted in Matthew 12:40?"

The problem is that you and I do not count the way the ancients counted. We nearly always count *exclusively;* they nearly always counted *inclusively.* I noticed in Latin III (ninth grade) that the letters of Cicero were dated funnily (at least according to my sensibilities). I routinely found phrases like, "The fifth day *after* the first of the month." To the ancient Romans—get this!—that meant the fifth of the month. We of course would read it as the sixth. But they counted inclusively; they counted the first *and* last items in a series. (They counted the way many of us did when we were children!) Thus the fifth day after the first, for them, was the fifth. Of course I protested to my Latin teacher, but to no avail. I found the same to be the case with ancient Greek and even ancient Hebrew documents. Like it or not, the ancients counted differently than we do.

That is how one gospel can say "after three days," another records Jesus as saying "on the third day," and yet the meaning is the same in each case. Friday—Saturday—Sunday is three days; and Sunday is "three days" after Friday.

This brings up something very interesting in how the amount of time passed is described with the words *days* and *nights.* We would consider *three days and three nights* to be seventy-two hours or so, since both *nights* and *days* are mentioned. One day and one night is twenty-four hours, and twenty-four times three is seventy-two. But we could also describe the same amount of time as *three days*: "I stayed in town three days" obviously includes at least two nights, possibly three. To the Hebrews, *a day* usually meant a night and a day. Thus *three days* means three nights and three days, approximately seventy-two hours. But it could equally well (as in this case) signify one night, a day, another night and part of the following morning—scarcely thirty-six hours! The distinction is important; you will come across this anomaly a number of times in the Scriptures. (See also *The Bible on Trial*, question 5a.)

18. Kill the Heathen?

"Why were the chosen people of God in the Old Testament told to destroy all the nations in the promised land as they entered it, not sparing men, women or children, whereas in the New Testament we are called to make disciples of all nations? Human nature has not changed, has it? So why weren't the Israelites told to convert the lost cultures, teaching them to repent of their sins and turn to God?"

You have noticed a major difference between the two testaments. The Old Testament, which is much more "physical," instituted a "state church": the people of God were one unit spiritually as well as *politically*. Under the New Testament or new covenant, church and state are separate. Let me put it another way: under the first covenant, whatever the people of God did, the government was doing. These days, we have no such authority to collect taxes, wage war, apportion land, etc. And through Israel, the people of God under the Old Testament, the Lord was punishing the Canaanites.

Several considerations are germane to this discussion:

- The Israelites were not chosen to punish the Canaanites because of their own virtue (Deuteronomy 9:4-6).
- Canaanite sin commonly included child sacrifice, male and female temple prostitution, incest and more! (See Leviticus 18.) This was a heartless society and

their influence on Israel, God knew, would be sufficient to drag the new nation into spiritual darkness.
Later, this is exactly what happened, as we see in
the book of Judges. Israel only partially broke away
from "the world." She even intermarried with the
Canaanites and other pagan nations, as we see in
Ezra and Nehemiah!

- The Canaanites as a whole were beyond reforming.
  For example, in the major city of Jericho, what was
  the occupation of the most righteous person? Rahab
  was a prostitute!

- Deuteronomy 20 contains important instructions on
  how (politically) Israel was to approach certain pagan cities. Notice the sharp distinction between the
  Canaanites and the surrounding nations. There was
  to be no relationship with the Canaanites, but other
  nations were to be offered terms of peace.

- In the spirit of Exodus 19:6, the Israelites *did* in fact
  convert a number of people because of their example, such as Rahab. The people of God under
  both covenants had the same purpose: to enjoy a
  relationship with God. And yet *their* mission is not
  equivalent to *ours*.

19. Exodus 4:24

"In Exodus 4:24, why was God going to kill Moses right
after God gave him specific direction? Why was he going to
kill his son?"

God was going to kill Moses' son, not Moses himself. The
Hebrew says that God was going to kill "him," following the
threat to kill the firstborn son in verse 23. Presumably he
was going to kill his son because Moses had failed to cir-
cumcise him, despite the clear teaching on circumcision going
back to Genesis 17. (Notice that this is exactly what Zipporah,
Moses' wife, who apparently had a problem with God's
command, does to their son, and so God left him alone,
related in verses 24-25.)

20. 1 Samuel 28:3-17

"Can the medium or spiritist bring back the spirits of the dead? Or is it that a demon was impersonating Samuel?"

Based on 1 Samuel 28, apparently mediums *have* successfully contacted the dead; 1 Samuel 28 says nothing about a demon. If necromancy (consulting the dead) is only a trick, it is hard to explain the warnings against it such as we find in Deuteronomy.

So, as for the witch of Endor, it appears (to me, at least) that she truly *was* calling up Samuel from the dead. Can people do this today? Can spiritists in Africa break through to the other side? Though I am extremely skeptical, I must say that I honestly do not know.

In my understanding, the dead are conscious, though they prefer not to be "disturbed."[2]

21. John 20:22-23

"John 20:22-23 reads (NLT), 'And with that he breathed on them and said, "Receive the Holy Spirit. If you forgive anyone his sins, they are forgiven; if you do not forgive them, they are not forgiven."' What's the reason for Jesus' breathing on them? Does this relate to Matthew 16:19? Was this promise for the apostles alone or for all believers? Jesus had the power on earth to forgive sins. Did the apostles have that same power? How does Jesus' sacrifice fit with this scripture?"

I have taken John 20:22 to be a dramatic action indicating the apostles were at that time (or possibly at a later time) to receive the Spirit. It seems to tie in with Matthew 16. In the case of the apostles (who were right with God before Pentecost—John 15 says they were already clean by the word Jesus had spoken), they received special abilities and privileges that do not pertain to all believers. (See Luke 9:2; John 14:26, 16:13; Acts 2:42-43; etc.) The apostles never remitted sins on earth, as Jesus did in Mark 2. Jesus helped people to get right with God under the old covenant. From Pentecost on, the apostles helped people to be saved through the new covenant, entailing repentance and baptism.

22. Luke 22 and the Sword

"Regarding response to enemies, the question for me seems to be not so much attacking one's enemies, but using force in defense of the oppressed or vulnerable. For example in East Timor last year, the Indonesian army was sanctioning mass genocide and clearly the only way to prevent that was through sending in the UN peacekeeping forces. Similarly, what do you do if your wife and family are being attacked? In such a situation you couldn't be expected just to stand by. Passively allowing yourself to be maimed or killed isn't going to help them either. Where is the line drawn? Is it just in the immediate defense of people, or is the defense of principles okay?

Also, although Jesus clearly preaches to turn the other cheek, he is not totally anti-violence. In Luke 22:36-51 Jesus tells his followers to sell their cloaks and buy swords. Then when one of them uses his sword (Peter, according to John 18), Jesus tells them to stop—but obviously did not prevent it from happening."

In regard to your first question, the highest principle—which can override other principles—is *love*. While we never wish to hurt our enemies, we love our families (for example) more and must do what our consciences impel us to do to protect them. I have no comment on the UN action in East Timor because the New Testament does not comment on secular military action.

As for Luke 22, this passage has been the source of much lively discussion in the past two millennia! (Have you read the commentaries on the passage?) Some commentators think Jesus advocated carrying arms, yet most think he was misunderstood (as in, "From now on, things are going to get hot. The thing you'd benefit from is not extra clothing, but protection."). As William Barclay puts it,

...Jesus was saying, "All the time so far you have had me with
you. In a very short time you are going to be cast upon your
own resources. What are you going to do about it? The danger
in a very short time is not that you will possess nothing; but that
you will have to fight for your very existence." This was not an
incitement to armed force. It was simply a vivid Eastern way of
telling the disciples that their very lives were at stake.[3]

As so often happened, the disciples took their Lord *literally*, completely misunderstanding his words. He chides
them, "Enough"—as in, "enough of this"; moreover, he heals
the man whose ear Peter lopped off. No, violence was not
the way of the Master.

And as for Jesus' preventing violence from taking
place—well, God does not prevent violence. Rather, he
brings good out of bad situations. He helps us to pick up
the broken pieces.

23. 1 Kings 13

"In 1 Kings 13 did the man of God sin, or was he simply
deceived? If he was deceived, wasn't then his death a little
too tragic? What could he have done differently? When he
found out that he was deceived, his response (basically, no
response) is hard for me to understand or imagine. Can you
comment on that? What was the old prophet's thinking or
motivation through the whole incident? It does not make
sense to me, but I know God teaches us something here.
What is it? Or what are they?"

The answer to your question inheres in the theological point
of the passage. The young prophet went against the word
of the Lord—which is *never* permissible! Just as in Galatians
1:6-9, no one has the right to supersede the commands of
God. Sincerity was not the issue, and neither is sincerity the
issue today. There are many sincere religious persons today, religious but lost, because they are not following God's
will. (See Matthew 7:21-23.) As for the old prophet's motivation, the text does not say. It is interesting, though, that
the old prophet is from Bethel—site of idolatry among the

northern Israelites. God allowed the young prophet to be tested and unfortunately, he failed. A sobering lesson for all who read it!

24. The Two Thieves and Gospel Discrepancies

"My question has to do with the two thieves crucified with Jesus. I grew up believing that one cursed Jesus and the other asked for forgiveness. In Matthew and Mark it said that the thieves hurled insults at Jesus. Luke indicated that one thief hurled insults while the other asked for forgiveness, whereas John did not mention the thieves at all. I am not sure how I would go about explaining the differences, although I myself am quite comfortable with the way Luke records the event."

This is a good example of discrepancies or "surface contradictions" in the gospel accounts. It is a testimony to the integrity of the writers and compilers of the New Testament that minor discrepancies were allowed to stand. The temptation to blur the differences was surely there.

I myself see no problem in harmonizing a way to a solution: the thief who found salvation repented of his cursing while on the cross itself. Under extreme stress, people may allow words out of their mouths that would never be heard under normal circumstances. This explanation is not psychologically implausible, at any rate.

You ask why there are discrepancies. Differences in reporting the events exist in the Gospels because the Spirit is emphasizing different truths to us in the various passages. A few of my thoughts on the different emphases:

- The repentance of the thief, who was apparently a lower-class person, is important to the theology of Luke, who stresses the plight of the poor and their place in the kingdom of God. Similarly, Luke pays special attention to the situation of women in the world and in the life of Jesus, much more than the other evangelists (for example, in chapters 1, 7 and 8).

- This account is part of the inspired word of God, but Matthew, Mark and John did not include it. The gospel writers had to make decisions over what to include and perhaps even more, over what to exclude! (See the last verses of John.)

- If God had not intended to stress different points in the four gospels, he could have (and probably would have) given us just *one* gospel. Evidently the Spirit thought it important that we read each gospel with sensitivity to its distinctive focus.

- That the thief's last-minute conversion is passed over in the three other gospels should not concern us, for it is only peripheral to the concerns of the evangelists (the death of Jesus).

Finally, I think you would find Fee and Stuart's *How to Read the Bible for All Its Worth* extremely helpful—as would most of my readers. I strongly recommend this work.

25. Abimelech and Sarah

"Sometimes God confuses me in the Old Testament. For instance, take the whole chapter of Genesis 20 about Abraham and Abimelech. Here we read that for the second time Abraham gives his wife away as if she were his sister. It seems as if God's wrath is toward Abimelech. Yet he was marrying her with a 'clear conscience' (v5). God comes to Abimelech in a dream and says, 'Now return the man's wife, for he is a prophet, and he will pray for you and you will live' (v7). God never mentions Abraham's sin in the situation of deceit and giving his wife into potential adultery for the second time. But God does mention that Abraham, his prophet, will pray for Abimelech, who had a clear conscience. It just seems backward to me. Maybe you can shed some light on the passage."

The Bible certainly tells the story of all its characters without whitewashing. You are right. Here it is Abraham who is weakening in faith and telling a lie (or a half-truth, as Sarah was technically his half sister). And Abraham is reproached by the pagan king's behavior. Isn't it like that sometimes even for us in our Christian lives—times when nonbelievers may behave more "righteously" than we do? This is only to be expected, as we are all sinners, pagan and Christian alike. So it does indeed feel backward, for standards of conduct have been reversed.

But as for Abimelech's innocence in the sight of God, he *was* on the verge of marrying a woman who already had a husband. Having a clear conscience does not exempt us from guilt or responsibility (1 Corinthians 4:4). Abimelech took Sarah into his harem based on her looks alone; had he spent any time getting to know her, building a relationship, he would have soon discovered the truth of the matter.

26. 1 Corinthians 3:15

"I would like to have a better understanding on the matter of 1 Corinthians 3:13-15. In verse 15, how can someone be saved if his work hasn't passed the 'fire test'?"

As we read 1 Corinthians 3 in context, we see that the passage deals with church building, *not* our individual Christian lives (and certainly not purgatory, as the Roman church claims). Paul seems to be saying that if the foundation of the congregation you have built is unstable, your work will "burn up," though you will still be saved. So unless you are a church builder, the "fire test" does not apply to you.

As for whether you can be saved if your life's work does not "pass the test"—well, we rightly reject salvation by works. Of course God's grace produces in us a rejection of worldliness (Titus 2:11-14) and a determination to work hard (1 Corinthians 15:10), but we do not work *in order to* be saved. We don't have to "measure up." Isn't this good news? Enjoy your salvation!

27. Jeremiah 8:7

"I was reading Jeremiah 8:7-8 (which accuses the scribes of falsely handling the Scriptures) and had several questions about the role of the scribes. Were the scribes responsible for wrongly copying Scripture? Or were they responsible for teaching incorrectly or only selectively the Scriptures? Please clear up the role of the scribes and how the 'lying pen' of the scribes should be viewed."

I have often read Jeremiah 8 and wondered the same sorts of things. You are right to consider *several* possible answers to the question before deciding you know what the passage means. Although the scribes copied the Torah faithfully, they twisted the Scriptures to their own destruction, as Jeremiah laments. (See also 2 Peter 3:16.) Any time a leader misrepresents God, it is a very serious thing.

28. Hebrews 8—Bible Teaching Necessary?

"Does Hebrews 8:10-11 mean that we will no longer have to teach people the Bible because they'll already know the Lord?"

Not at all! Hebrews 8 is describing the difference between the old covenant, in which people normally entered the covenant apart from their will (as babies), and the new covenant, in which only as responsible, believing, repentant individuals do we begin our relationship with God. The problem of the Old Testament was that people struggled greatly with their commitment when it was their parents who had made their decisions for them. Jesus showed us a different way; no longer would we be born into the church. Your parents cannot decide for you (John 1:13).

I realize that in one sense, we all benefit from Bible teaching and deeply need it—we don't know enough just because we are baptized—but this isn't the subject of Hebrews 8.

To summarize, in Judaism you had to be taught to know the Lord because you knew nothing about him when you became a Jew. In Christianity, on the other hand, you have been instructed beforehand and you know what you are getting into.

29. Child Sacrifice

"In Leviticus 18:21, Deuteronomy 12:31, 2 Kings 16:3 and Ezekiel 16:20-21, God seems to express an extraordinary disgust for the practice of child sacrifice. Could you please help me understand why he chose this method, child sacrifice, to reconcile us to him?"

You have put your finger on an amazing paradox, one seldom noticed by most Christians! A good question, especially considering that child sacrifice was so common in OT times, and God so strongly forbid it. Here are my thoughts:

- I would not call the death of Jesus a child sacrifice because, although Jesus was God's Son, he was not a child when he was sacrificed. He voluntarily submitted his will to the Father's will. (See Matthew 26, especially vv52-54 and John 18:11.) The abhorrent custom of child sacrifice was normally applied to infants. Incidentally, some have suggested that God "murdered" Jesus. Yet this sort of language does not appear in the Bible; it is an inference that does not redound well to God's character.
- The death of Jesus was an offering *by God* made *to God.* The deaths of multitudes of babies in OT times (for example, as sacrifices to Molech) were made *by man to a false (nonexistent) god.*
- The pagans believed that giving up their firstborn, like offering firstfruits, was essential to agriculture and fertility. Canaanite religions, for example, revolved around weather and farming. Jesus' death, however, brought no such temporal benefit.
- The crucifixion of Jesus Christ was more than the death of a man; it was the experience of death, in some sense, of God. Acts 20:28 reads, "...the church

of God, which he bought with his own blood." No man could ever die for the sins of another, as Psalm 49:7-8 clearly says. In this vital respect, the death of Jesus was totally unlike any child sacrifice in history.

• Finally, as a matter of interest, the death of Jesus was foreshadowed in the "sacrifice" of Isaac (Genesis 22). Actually, neither was ultimately lost: Isaac was saved by a substitution, while Jesus was rescued through resurrection. In a way, in each offering God is showing that he does not desire the destruction of a child.

Notes

¹ You will find my original view in *Life to the Full*, 80-89.

² For more thoughts on this, see archived question 60a in *The Bible on Trial*, as well as my book *The Spirit* (e.g. chapter 28).

³ William Barclay, *Daily Study Bible Series: The Gospel of Luke*, rev. ed. (Philadelphia: Westminster/John Knox, 1975), 269-270.

3
Basic Bible

1. Incarnation

"Which passages would you use to show that Jesus is God in the flesh, and what would you say in support of those passages?"

One of the best is certainly John 1:14. The Word (John 1:1) became flesh; and this Word is God. Yet there are many other passages that are clear: Colossians 1, Philippians 2, Hebrews 1-2, etc. The theological term for God becoming man is "incarnation," which could also be rendered "enfleshment": God taking on humanity—arguably the greatest miracle of the Bible—the Almighty spanning an infinite chasm to reach you and me, Creator reaching out to creature.

2. Communion

"I have always had some questions about Acts 2:42. The question I have is whether their devotion to the 'breaking of the bread' is referring to eating meals with each other or the taking of the Lord's Supper?"

As you have noticed, the phrase "breaking of bread" is somewhat ambivalent; it could actually mean either. Only in context can it be determined whether it refers to the Lord's Supper or not. My take on Acts 2 is this: 2:42 refers to the Lord's Supper, while 2:46 refers to more ordinary fellowship meals.

It seems from the New Testament (Acts 20:7) and the early Christian sources that the early disciples celebrated the Lord's Supper regularly, probably weekly, but possibly more often.

3. Communion Questions

"Having grown up in the Catholic church, I am now studying the subject of the Lord's Supper. Do we have to make our worship in the communion time be with the really cheap crackers and generally less than ten minutes in length, compared with the one to one and one-half hours of preaching? And could you please give me some insight on how to understand that the bread is not actually turning into his body (that is to say, flesh) and the wine into his actual blood, as I was brought up to believe?"

Well, I have no comment on the "really cheap crackers," other than that we usually observe the tradition of following the Jewish Passover usage of unleavened bread. Jesus never explicitly told us what to use for the bread, so presumably this is an area of liberty.

As for the length of communion, again, the Bible does not say how long this should be or even whether it should be the longest part of our church services. I do sympathize with you if you really have to sit through sixty to ninety minutes of preaching *every* Sunday. (Now and again a longer message is nice, but as they say, "The mind can only take in as much as the seat can endure"!) Personally, I appreciate a meaningful time of communion. And as is the case with sermons, length is seldom related to quality.

Finally, as for the doctrine of transubstantiation, there are several problems if the bread and wine are *literally* the flesh and blood of Christ:

- In John 6 Jesus is speaking about the bread and wine, yet he is physically present with the disciples. How could the communion elements be his body if his body was at the table with the twelve disciples?
- Drinking blood was strictly against Jewish law.
- If transubstantiation is true, then at every "Mass," Christ is "sacrificed" again—whereas the book of Hebrews is emphatic that the sacrifice of Christ was "once for all," never to be repeated.

4. James, the Brother of Jesus

"How can we as Bible students tell the difference between characters in the Bible with the same first names for example, James, the brother of Jesus, and James, the brother of the apostle John? I usually rely on the commentary of chain references when the answer is not apparent. Also, I have heard before that James, the brother of Jesus, was executed. I understand that the execution of James in the book of Acts is referring to the apostle James. Was James, the brother of Jesus, executed? If so, where do I find this, in the Bible or in another text?"

Your method of using a commentary or following chain references will nearly always clear up any confusion about who's who. "James" is an interesting case, since there are many Jameses in the Bible (see if you can find all the others)!

Both of the Jameses you mention were martyred. James bar Zebedee, the apostle, is indicated in Acts 12—execution by the Roman sword means beheading. The later martyrdom of James the Just, the brother of Jesus, is mentioned by the first century Jewish historian Josephus.[1]

5. John the Baptist

"In Matthew 17:10-12 Jesus alludes to the fact that John the Baptist was the Elijah to come, yet in John 1:21 John the Baptist denies it. Is this because the Bible says in Malachi that a prophet was to come in the spirit of Elijah, rather than Elijah himself? Was John's denial a way to steer his disciples away from the idea of an actual reincarnation?"

Yes, this is exactly how I see the situation. Many Jews expected Elijah *literally* to return to the earth—and this notion continues to be part of Jewish tradition even today when the empty seat is left at the Seder Supper for Elijah. And John does come in the spirit (and clothing) of Elijah, his ninth century BC counterpart. There is no reincarnation Biblically (Job 7:9-10, Hebrews 9:27).

6. Melchizedek

"Many theologians, from what I have heard, have gone so far as to say that Melchizedek may have actually been Jesus. Can you shed any light on this subject for me?"

The Bible never says Jesus is Melchizedek, though there are several parallels. (I actually don't know of any theologians who have made this claim.) Melchizedek was a priest as well as a royal figure—just like Jesus. Melchizedek's priesthood—and this is the main point the Hebrew writer makes—was outside the usual order of things. If Jesus were a regular Jewish priest, he would have had to be from the tribe of Levi, but he was from Judah. Melchizedek functions as a precedent, a legitimate, respected priesthood prior to and outside the order established by God under the Old Covenant.

7. Women Preaching

"Can women 'share' in church? It seems to say in 1 Corinthians 14:34-35 that women should remain silent. Also, in 1 Timothy 2:11-12, again women should learn in silence. I know sharing is not teaching, but according to these scriptures it seems that women should be silent. Can you provide us with some insight?"

Yes, I would be happy to help. There is certainly a difference between preaching and sharing. One is appropriate in the assembly and enhances church services considerably. The other is out of place and breeds disunity. Generally, in the churches I am most closely associated with, we discourage the sisters from reading the Bible or exhorting the assembly, based on 1 Corinthians 14. The question is, what kind of "silence" does Paul have in mind? It could not be total silence since in 1 Corinthians 11 we see that the women were allowed to pray in the assembly.

In 1990 I coauthored a paper with Pat Gempel on the role of women. This paper is suitable for sharing with your friends who don't necessarily fully trust the inspiration of the Bible. It is found in the final section of this book, along with several other longer essays. But to answer your question, yes, women may share. But unfortunately many women, in the absence of clear guidelines from leaders, do in my judgment, "cross the line."

8. Taxpaying

"In Matthew 17:27 Jesus gives instructions to Peter to go fish for the temple tax and to give it so as not to offend the Pharisees. But Jesus was not one to be concerned about offending or not offending the Pharisees. So what is his real message in this?"

Another great question. Let me say at the outset that I do pay my taxes and so should you—not just in order not to offend, but because it's right (Romans 13). We can distinguish two taxes in the New Testament: those paid to the state (the government) and those paid to the "church" (the temple and its priesthood). Jesus does not fully accept the legitimacy of the Jewish religious system, which explains why he pays the tax in order to not offend them. We, however, don't pay taxes so as not to offend the governing authorities! Notice that the coin pays the tax for Peter and Jesus—both pay. Unlike so many leaders of the day, Jesus did not make an exception of himself. There was one standard. There is still just one standard.

9. David's Census

"Who incited David to take the census? The Bible says in 2 Samuel that God incited David, and 1 Chronicles says that Satan incited David."

God (2 Samuel 24) and Satan (1 Chronicles 21) work in the same event. Does your view of God's will and providence conflict with this understanding? Another example is the crucifixion. According to Acts 2, although Satan seemed to score first, Jesus was crucified by the will of God. While they are not in league with each other, what Satan meant for evil, God was able to use for good (as in Genesis 50:20). (A similar dynamic may explain Job 1.)

This explanation will not satisfy until we understand one further fact. In the Old Testament very often events are attributed *directly* to the Lord even though he has only *indirectly* caused them. (Academics would call this the attribution of primary causation when only secondary causation is in effect.) In other words, what God *allows*—such as sickness, death, even sin—is sometimes described as though God *caused* it. Everything, after all, is either done by God or permitted by God, right? So the answer to the question of who caused David to order the census, God or Satan, is "both."

By the way, David's stubborn reliance on statistics, instead of relying on God to build and preserve the kingdom, was deeply unspiritual! Even Joab (the head of David's army and hardly a paragon of spirituality) found the orders repugnant. A heavy price was paid, and plague ultimately reduced the numbers of Israel, presumably in part because the census tax was not paid (see Exodus 30:12). See also question 8 in "Difficult Passages."

10. Calling of the Disciples

"Matthew and Mark describe the calling of the first disciples in similar accounts. Would Luke be considered a more descriptive version of those accounts? Would John's account be considered to have occurred before the synoptic versions?"

Matthew, Mark and Luke share a common outlook on the life and words of Christ; they are called the "synoptic" Gospels. However, the gospel of John is quite different, having fewer common links with the other three. Luke's is the longest and most descriptive of the four gospels, as well as stylistically the finest literary specimen. Luke was apparently a highly educated and eloquent physician (Colossians 4:14). As far as the time of composition of John's account, scholars are divided between those who place it late in the first century and those who place it earlier than the synoptics. Either position may be justifiable in light of the evidence we have.

If your question concerns John 1 versus Matthew 4, Mark 1 and Luke 5, then yes, John is recording a previous encounter with Jesus, which seems fairly obvious through even a cursory reading of the accounts. In other words, the calling of the fishermen to become fishers of men (Mark 1) was not a suggestion out of the blue to men Jesus had never met. If we are interpreting it that way and failing to build relationships (John 1) before issuing the challenge (Mark 1), then we are failing to emulate the example of Jesus— and we will fail to win over the broad spectrum of people that God wants us to reach with the gospel.

11. Judas' Suicide

"What is the explanation for Judas hanging himself (Matthew 27:5) versus falling headfirst and his intestines falling out (Acts 1:18)? I suppose it might be decomposition for the guts part, but what about the 'headlong' aspect?"

Quite a graphic question, not to mention the events themselves to which it refers! There are several possible harmonies, and I will leave it to you to work out the details. If you need some hints, see chapter 7 of my book *True and Reasonable*. And remember, hanging did not necessarily involve a rope in ancient times.

The fact that it is somewhat challenging to harmonize Matthew's and Luke's accounts is a testimony to the integrity of the early Christians, who chose not to tidy up the two accounts, but to leave them intact. Even in the newspapers today, firsthand accounts of identical events often lead to variations of detail and emphasis.

12. Gifts of the Spirit

"I have always been troubled by Acts 8:14-19. One explanation I have been told is that the Holy Spirit discussed here means only the miraculous gifts of the Spirit, not the indwelling Spirit. However, I have a hard time seeing this myself, much less proving it to someone else. Please help!"

I would encourage you to read my book *The Spirit*, which covers this issue in some detail. For now, let me give you my reasoning on this. In this passage the Spirit came visibly, and the magician wanted the power to perform this "trick." This does not describe what happened when you and I became Christians, does it?

Second, the text says that these men and women had already been baptized into the name of Jesus. Yet Acts 2:38 states that when someone is baptized in the name of Jesus, he receives the gift of the Spirit, and 2:39 avers that this is God's plan for all whom he will call. There are no exceptions, in other words. The Samaritans were already saved, forgiven *and* possessing the Spirit, since without the Spirit, you are not a Christian (Romans 8:9). This is why I am convinced that when Acts mentions the Spirit coming *on* them, it is referring to something different from the indwelling Spirit, which they had received upon responding to the message Philip preached.

13. Angel Wings

"On page 125 of your book, *Life to the Full*, you said that angels are 'never described as having wings,' yet Isaiah 6:2 describes the seraphs as having six wings. Were you referring to humanoid angels, or was that a mistake?"

Seraphs and cherubs are types of guardian spirits described in the Old Testament. "Regular" angels normally appear as humans; in fact, they are most often indistinguishable from them. As far as we can tell, angels (or "messengers"—Hebrew *malak* and Greek *angelos* both mean "angel" or "messenger") do not have wings. The archangel Gabriel being in "swift flight" in Daniel 9:21 does not prove he had wings.

14. Sabbath

"What is the truth behind the fourth commandment concerning the Sabbath? If Saturday is the seventh day and the Sabbath, why do we not worship on Saturday? If we observe Sunday as our 'Sabbath,' are we going against God's commandment?"

You are right that the seventh day is Saturday, and if we have to follow the Sabbath, Saturday is it. (Actually, the Sabbath is from sundown Friday to sundown Saturday—in the Old Testament and even in Israel today.) But Christians are never commanded to observe the Sabbath. In fact, the opposite is the case (Colossians 2:16-18).

If you would like an excellent book on the subject, let me recommend the thin volume by Anthony A. Hoekema, *Seventh Day Adventism.*[2] It was many centuries after the start of the church before Christians felt constrained to observe any kind of a Sabbath. In ancient times, Sunday was a workday, and so (in the early second century, at least) the disciples met at dawn and again in the evening on Sunday.

15. Salvation Under the Old Covenant

"What has always puzzled me is the salvation of the righteous under the Old Covenant. How were Moses, Abraham, David, et al. forgiven? If through faith in Christ (looking forward to the Messiah who would save them, as opposed to us looking back at the Christ who saves us), then how did they come into contact with the blood of Christ if they weren't baptized? Did they somehow gain forgiveness through the Old Covenant procedures and sacrifices God had instituted? And by the way, was John's baptism for forgiveness or just for repentance? I would be most grateful to get this cleared up."

How were people forgiven under the Old Covenant, since Hebrews 10:4 says that "it is impossible for the blood of bulls and goats to take away sins"? You have correctly surmised that their salvation must have been granted in some roundabout way, and I would like to offer an analogy that I think will throw some light on the matter.

Doug owes Steve ten thousand rand. Doug cannot afford to make the payment now, but he has a good friend, Joshua, who is willing to help out. Joshua tells Steve, "Hey,

I promise to pay you the ten thousand rand that Doug owes you." Steve is happy, though the price is yet to be paid. Doug is very happy. Here is the point: even though the price has not *yet* been paid, debtor, Doug, is released from his debt on the basis of the *word* of the one who will pay. The OT saints were saved through Jesus—and when he came to the earth and died, the "promissory note" was paid in full. Because of the power and integrity of Jesus' word, these men and women of faith were released from their debt of sin.

As for John the Baptist, who ministered in the final years of the Old Covenant, Mark 1:4 affirms that his baptism did indeed confer forgiveness of sins. That is, the erring people of God were in fact restored to their relationship with him. However, there was one enormous difference between his baptism and the baptism in Jesus' name—John's baptism did not bring the Holy Spirit. (See Acts 19:1-6.)

16. Negative Claims About the Truth of the Bible

"One time I stopped and talked to a girl who was taking some philosophy and religion courses at a university. She was studying the first century church and doubted the accuracy of the books written by Jesus' very own disciples because of the time lapse. I pointed out that Scripture is 'God breathed.' What more could be said? She also said that there were other books that were not included in the New Testament and wanted to know why they were left out. I had not heard of this before, and I was not prepared to speak on it. I have not read your book, *True and Reasonable*. I think I need to!"

Yes, I would encourage you to read *True and Reasonable*, as I think it will answer your questions. Using 2 Timothy 3:16 with an unbeliever is likely to fail if you are trying to convince her of the truth of the Bible. Many books claim inspiration, such as the Qur'an (Koran) and the Book of

Mormon. The conclusion Bible-believers have come to is stated in 2 Timothy 3:16, but it does nothing to convince an outsider or skeptic.

By the way, the time lapse between the time the New Testament books were written (by about 70 AD) and the earliest surviving manuscripts is quite small—only two generations, not 500 or 1000 years, as is the case with most works from antiquity.

17. Canonization

"Could you recommend a book about the history of the Bible? I mean, how it was decided which books and letters were the Bible? How do I know which scriptures (like in Isaiah or Psalms) are prophecies about the Messiah and which ones are not? I always wonder how people figure this out."

Many books, including *True and Reasonable,* have been written to clarify this matter. One of them that I highly recommend is Neil Lightfoot's *How We Got the Bible, Second Edition* (Grand Rapids: Baker, 1988), which I think is a must for your library. As for discerning which prophecies are messianic, why not take a look at the archived material in *The Bible on Trial.* There are a number of units on this very subject.

18. Commentaries

"It would be great if you could recommend a book or commentary or two on each book in the Bible, plus some general dictionaries. There are so many commentaries and books out there, and I have no idea whose is the most useful."

A commentary is a book that expounds on a book of the Bible, verse by verse, and considers all the significant possibilities as to how to understand the verses. Few disciples I've met have ever read a commentary, though these are valuable tools for Bible study. (To date no one in the International Churches of Christ has written a true commentary, which is not to be confused with Biblical exposition—as in DPI's *Practical Exposition Series.*)

If you're starting out, the *Daily Study Bible* series by Barclay is not bad, and many Christians have enjoyed reading it. The reader does need to understand that Barclay often takes a humanistic view of miracles. The volumes are inexpensive. Most commentaries are more costly. Perhaps the best commentary series available today is *The Word* series. Expect to pay twenty-five to thirty dollars per volume. The Tyndale Old Testament Commentaries (Inter-Varsity Press) and the Tyndale New Testament Commentaries (Eerdmans Publishing Co.) are available in paperback and are a reliable and more inexpensive alternative.

Another observation about commentary series is that they tend to be of uneven quality. Because a different scholar takes each book of the Bible, some are better written (and closer to the truth) than others. I would consider buying based on the writer, more than on the series itself. (Fun note: one series, not "serie" or two series; "series" is both singular and plural.)

Finally, here are two books for selecting the right commentaries for you. They are, so to speak, commentaries about commentaries.

- D. A. Carson, *A New Testament Commentary Survey, Fourth Edition* (Downers Grove, Illinois: InterVarsity, 1993).
- Tremper Longman III, *Old Testament Commentary Survey, Second Edition* (Grand Rapids: Baker Books, 1995).

No further comment!

19. The Nephilim

"Who were the Nephilim?"

The term literally means "the fallen ones." Some say they were a race of giants, the offspring of angels and women, to which Goliath and Lahmi (1 Chronicles 20:5) belonged. This sounds too much like Greek, Roman and Norse mythology for me. Others say they were the sinful seed of Cain, who later appear as the Canaanites. Scholarship is divided, with the majority taking them to be a race of giants. One interesting matter is that the Bible says (Genesis 6) that they were on the earth in the days before the Flood—"and afterward." What does *that* mean?

I have shared my own thoughts in *The God Who Dared*, which is a book on Genesis 1-11. Do read the footnotes as well as the main text, and have fun.

20. Go Make Disciples

"What is Jesus commanding us to do in the Great Commission?"

After his death and resurrection, Jesus gave the charge, the "Great Commission," to the eleven faithful apostles. Let's take a look at this passage and see what we can conclude.

> Then Jesus came to them and said, "All authority in heaven and on earth has been given to me. Therefore go and make disciples of all nations, baptizing them in the name of the Father and of the Son and of the Holy Spirit, and teaching them to obey everything I have commanded you. And surely I am with you always, to the very end of the age." (Matthew 28:18-20)

God wants the world to be evangelized. It is his will that everyone on the planet have a chance to meet a messenger who will share the good news. The Commission triggers a chain reaction as disciples replicate themselves in obedience to the command. This action process is the church. A true church consists of disciples making disciples making disciples…!

Yet "make disciples" is translated from only one word in Greek. An alternative and equally correct rendering would be "disciple the nations." While "disciple" is common as a noun, it is quite rare as a verb, and so most translators opt for the two-word construction "make disciples."

Baptism is set in the context of discipleship. No one who is unready to give his or her life to the Lord in discipleship is a true candidate for baptism.

The "them" (verse 19) refers, in context, to "the nations," not to "disciples." We are to call the nations to discipleship and baptism. This is not to say one does not need to be ready to become a disciple before baptism. But in Matthew 28 we are called to disciple (teach), baptize and further instruct the nations.

Obedience (verse 20) must be *taught*. It isn't natural! Our job as disciples is therefore not only to evangelize the world, but also to keep the teaching process going in our churches.

As we obey the Commission, Jesus gives his word that he will be with us always. Let's give ourselves heart and soul to the Great Commission, urgently carrying out the request of Jesus Christ!

21. Baptizing Disciples

"Doesn't the Bible teach that 'disciple' is another word for 'Christian' (Acts 11:26)? Is Jesus really saying we are to baptize disciples—those who are already in a right relationship with God?"

The ambiguity arises because, like many words, the word "disciple" has different nuances. "Disciple" is the standard term for a follower of Jesus, appearing some thirty times in the book of Acts alone. Denominational Christianity has substituted the world's term, "Christian," for the Biblical term, "disciple." They claim that being a disciple is a more committed Christian, but the two-tier model of discipleship is not the plan Jesus set up.

On the other hand, in ancient times (and modern) many men had disciples. In this case the word "disciple" is a rather general term. (John 4:1 probably illustrates this sense of the word.)

Among modern-day disciples, the word also often describes the *attitude* of one eager to follow Jesus. This attitude is part of Biblical repentance.

So, we must understand in which sense the word is being used: "disciple" as one already saved, "disciple" as a follower (of whoever) or "disciple" as one aspiring to total commitment to Jesus Christ as Lord. This is not to encourage semantic haggling, but the fact remains that words are often used in different senses.

However we prefer to use the word, the text of Matthew 28:19 teaches that we are to baptize the nations (that is, the men and women of all nations). It is at the point of conversion (not before) that they become true disciples of Jesus Christ.

22. Enemies

"I'm curious about how to reconcile Jesus' attitude toward enemies with the Old Testament's attitude. Further, I'm curious as to how a Christian is to view the maintenance of a standing army to protect a country's way of life. Can a Christian soldier ever attack an enemy?"

This question brings us into waters seldom plowed by the vessels of our Biblical investigation! In Matthew 5 Jesus absolutely forbids us from being uncharitable toward our enemies. In Matthew 7 he adds that we are to do to others as we would have them do to us. This means it is wrong for a Christian to abuse, kill or otherwise harm his enemy. (It's wrong even not to forgive them or pray for them, isn't it?) Accordingly, the early Christians chose consistently to be killed rather than to kill their enemies. This is not to say that there were not Christians in the imperial armies. Yet they had joined the army before baptism and after conversion refused to take up the sword, as their Lord enjoined them (Matthew 26:52).

As an American, I enjoy many privileges secured and preserved by our nation's standing army. I freely admit that nearly all the reasons for the powerful US military are economic. (As a younger man, I cherished a somewhat loftier and nobler view of politics.) Often I am deeply ashamed of the crass materialism behind much of the politics of our nation, especially when it masquerades as being honorable and noble. You asked me how I as a Christian view this standing army. I ask you a question: Was it the way of Jesus to use force to preserve his life, let alone his "way of life"?

Finally, under the Old Covenant, the church and state were one, and on some occasions warfare was tolerated or even commanded (see Deuteronomy 20). But today we as a church are *separate* from the state, and the way of Christ is not political (John 6:15, 18:36).

Around 400 AD, after the fires of persecution abated and church and state became one again (the Holy Roman Empire), killing one's enemies was authorized (so was torturing "heretics"—those who disagreed with the church party line). During the Reformation (1500s), Luther and Calvin brought the church back to the fourth century (not the first, as they claimed), by approving of killing. This has remained the mainline Protestant position ever since.

I believe you would appreciate John Driver's little book on Christians and the military, *How Christians Made Peace with War,*[3] though I urge you to study the Bible for yourself and come to your own conclusions on the matter.

23. Quarreling

"I have been advised that it is pretty useless studying with Jehovah's Witnesses because they are stubborn and nothing will eventuate. Surely there has to be an effective way to study with Jehovah's Witnesses without it ending in self-righteousness and arguments. How would you go about doing it?"

Let me say first of all that Witnesses *have* been converted to Christ on several occasions. Though this is a much rarer event than we would hope for, it is totally possible to bring a sincerely seeking Witness to a knowledge of the truth. Let us take the advice of Paul, who wrote to Timothy about some of the pitfalls of arguments.

> Keep reminding them of these things. Warn them before God against quarreling about words; it is of no value, and only ruins those who listen. Do your best to present yourself to God as one approved, a workman who does not need to be ashamed and who correctly handles the word of truth.
> Don't have anything to do with foolish and stupid arguments, because you know they produce quarrels. And the Lord's servant must not quarrel; instead, he must be kind to everyone, able to teach, not resentful. Those who oppose him he must gently instruct, in the hope that God will grant them repentance leading them to a knowledge of the truth, and that they will come to their senses and escape from the trap of the devil, who has taken them captive to do his will. (2 Timothy 2:14-16, 23-26)

Salient points:

- Never quarrel about words.
- Be sure you know your stuff. Increasing your volume is no cover for poor Bible knowledge.
- No arguments.
- Be kind to the one who opposes you. Be nice!
- Instruct gently.
- Realize where people truly stand spiritually, and pray for God to work in their lives.

24. Iron and Clay

"In Daniel 2:43, Daniel explains that the toes of the statue King Nebuchadnezzar dreamed of were made partly of iron and partly of clay, meaning that the people of that kingdom would be divided and would not remain united. I have always thought that this referred to the political strife between the Romans and the Jews. However, I recently heard the view that this scripture is referring to intermarriage. Which is correct?"

Commentators offer different suggestions, but the dominant view is that the mixture of iron and clay refers to the mixture of Romans (iron = strength) and foreigners, or subject peoples (clay = weakness) in the Empire. Ultimately, iron and clay will not stay together, indicating internal weakness within the Empire. Defending the borders was always a vital need for the Romans—especially the eastern border. The armies were constantly needed to secure the provinces. This may well have involved intermarriage. It is not likely strife between Romans and Jews is in view.

25. Deaconesses?

"In 1 Timothy 3 the Scriptures talk about the standard of appointing a man as deacon. Appointing women as 'deaconesses' was not mentioned. Why? Is it a matter of opinion on our part to appoint women as 'deaconesses'?"

A valid question. Students of church history know that by the third century, the office of deaconess had developed. But what does the Bible teach? What was the practice of the first century church?

Support for this position is absent in the New Testament. In the International Churches of Christ our policy does not recognize an official position of "deaconess." Several years back, "deaconesses" actually were recognized, but when this was questioned on the basis of the teaching of the NT Scriptures (1998-99), a period of discussion ensued which led to a reversal of the policy. A possible passage supporting the deaconess concept is Romans 16:1, where Phoebe is said to be a deaconess/servant/minister of the church at Cenchrea. It is not at all clear that this is the female counterpart to the male deacon/servant/minister (depending on the translation) in 1 Timothy 3.

Where the Scriptures are silent we need to proceed cautiously. I am afraid we are on shaky ground if we claim the letters of Paul as support for an official office of deaconess.

Note: Special thanks must go to my friend Cecil Wooten for raising the question and launching the discussion on "deaconesses" in 1998 and 1999.

26. Jericho

"I've been taught that at the time the Israelites would have come upon Jericho, it was little more than an unfortified and very sparsely populated town, whereas the Biblical account makes it sound like a thriving, well-fortified place. How do I reconcile this with Scripture? Could it be that the archaeological research is wrong? Are there other possible and plausible dates for when Joshua would have come through this area (other than the fifteenth or thirteenth centuries BC) so as to match more correctly with the Biblical record? Or is there another way of reading the text here that would explain these apparent discrepancies?"

There are two major proposals for the dating of the conquest under Joshua: the late fifteenth century BC (approximately 1406) and the thirteenth century BC. Scholars are divided. So how you interpret the evidence will hinge somewhat on which century you believe the Bible indicates for the conquest. I believe the Biblical account is correct; Jericho was a major urban center and militarily, a strategic target for the invading Israelites (Joshua 6).

As for the population, the second city of the region was Ai (Joshua 7-8), which had a total of twelve thousand adult inhabitants (not impressive for a city population in our day). Jericho was certainly bigger. Does a city (town) of twenty-five or fifty thousand sound impressive? Probably not. In the eighth century BC, a much more significant power in the area was Assyria. Nineveh had some 120,000 inhabitants—ten times the size of Ai, perhaps several times the population of Jericho.

There are many great books to read on the subject, and I would point you to Steve Kinnard's column on Aces Online called *Digging Deeper*. In short, scholars often tend to minimize the truth content of the Scriptures. And yet such scoffing is not warranted.

27. Pauline Authorship

"I want to know what you think about the authorship of some of the NT books traditionally accepted as written by Paul. For instance, some scholars state that the books of Ephesians, 1 and 2 Timothy and Titus were definitely not written by Paul, and others (such as 2 Thessalonians and Colossians) probably weren't written by him. Also, some of the content of these letters seems to disclose the hope of Christ returning very quickly. Did Paul think that Jesus would return before his death?"

In the nineteenth century it was popular to date as many NT books in the second century as possible. The gospel of John, for example, was dated in the second half of the 100s—at least until papyri containing sections of the gospel of John were discovered from the first half of the century. In addition, it became quite popular to deny the reputed or explicit authorship of a document based on dubious stylistic arguments. Ephesians and 1 Timothy, which you ask about, were claimed to reflect a "later," "more advanced" stage in church history, at least a generation after the death of the "author" (Paul). Here again, there is a certain shallowness of argumentation, a certain overeagerness to reach conclusions. In the pastoral Epistles (1 and 2 Timothy and Titus), Paul writes as a church leader to another church leader. Wouldn't we expect different vocabulary, theological emphasis and agenda to what is typical of a letter to an entire church? For the most part, questions of authorship are easily resolved and the objections quickly undermined, once we probe deeper.

As for the expectation of the imminent return of Christ, opinion even among disciples is certainly divided. Many

passages borrow the language of judgment, yet are referring to the fall of Jerusalem (the "mini-Apocalypses" of the
Gospels) or even the fall of Rome (Revelation). The
wrongheaded understanding of an imminent end is rebuked
in 1 Thessalonians—by Paul himself. He urges us to settle
down, live responsibly and not become easily unsettled—in
both 1 and 2 Thessalonians.

28. Lamb of God

"I read somewhere that Jesus is called the 'Lamb of God' for
a specific reason. In John 1, John the Baptist calls Jesus the
'Lamb of God' and recognizes him even from a distance.
Now the Jews were sacrificing animals at the time of the
crucifixion, and Jesus was sacrificed as the 'Lamb of God.'
Was the name significant at that time, and also, was his
crucifixion at that time also significant?"

I don't know whether the appellation "Lamb of God" was
significant at the time or not, in terms of being a technical
term. Of course it's loaded with Passover significance, and
it is no mere coincidence that Jesus was crucified that week.
Many books have been written on this subject.

29. Holy Spirit

"I have a question about baptism and receiving the gift of
the Holy Spirit. There are certainly numerous accounts in
the Bible indicating that baptism is an integral part of salvation. Can you explain a situation like in Acts 10:44-45, where
the 'Holy Spirit came on all who heard the message,' and
then they were baptized?"

Yes, on the surface of things, Acts 10 seems to allow salvation before baptism, while Acts 8 does just the opposite,
whereas Acts 2:39 indicates that repentance and baptism
are conditions for receiving forgiveness and the Spirit
unchangingly, for all generations.

The natural conclusion, considering that Peter had only just *begun* to deliver the saving message (Acts 11:15), is that their knowledge was, as of that point, insufficient. In other words, they did not receive the *indwelling* of the Spirit. For more on this, please see my book *The Spirit*, chapter 18, which deals explicitly with your questions.

30. Tongues 1

"I would like to hear your take, Biblically, on speaking in tongues and why this is not practiced in the kingdom today. My other question is about the offices of leadership in the church. Why are there no more apostles or prophets?"

In the New Testament, "tongues" (languages) are actual human languages, as demonstrated in Acts 2:6-11. In the kingdom today people speak in many languages—many hundreds, in fact. Of course I am referring to normal foreign languages ("tongues"—the word is the same in the Greek). I personally have heard charismatics who claim to have the ability to speak in tongues, yet every time I have listened to them, I have remained unimpressed. At any rate, I think you may enjoy my book *The Spirit,* chapter 22, which deals exclusively with your question about tongues.

The word "apostle" can be used in a broader sense to refer to missionaries. However, it is used in the New Testament in a more specialized sense to apply to those who served as the unique leaders of the early church. There are no apostles today in that sense, because they were:

- eyewitnesses of the resurrection (Acts 1:22, 1 Corinthians 9:1).
- reminded by the Spirit of Jesus of the things he'd said to them (John 14:26, 16:13).
- inspired regarding their doctrine (Acts 2:42).

There are no church leaders today who are inspired to give us doctrine straight from God, nor were any of them alive twenty centuries ago, at the time of the resurrection of Jesus from the dead.

As for NT prophets (see Ephesians 2:20, 3:5, 4:11—all these passages discuss *New* Testament, not *Old* Testament prophets), they are long gone, too. The Bible, in Ephesians 2:20 (be sure to look up all these passages), explains that the apostles and prophets laid the foundation of the church in the first century. The foundation has been laid, hence it does not need to be laid again. As we follow their inspired words (found in the New Testament), we continue to build on that foundation. For more on this issue, and in particular about the unique roles of apostles and prophets, see my book *The Spirit*.

31. Tongues 2

"I've been studying out different religious doctrines for a while. One that I am looking for a stronger answer to is the practice of speaking in tongues. It's evident that the Bible does not declare that tongues is mandatory for salvation, nor was it ever. However, I'm curious as to how and why it died out. I know that one view is taken from 1 Corinthians 13: '...when perfection comes, the imperfect disappears.' But can that relate to this topic? How did the gift of tongues die out?"

You are right. According to 1 Corinthians 12:28-30, tongues (true languages) was no more essential for salvation than being an apostle was. The 1 Corinthians 13 argument may be true, but it is hardly satisfying. If you want to see why the Biblical gift of languages passed away, please see chapters 22 and 23 of my book *The Spirit*.

Since I have referred to it so often and will again, let me say something about my book, *The Spirit*. I wrote this book for two purposes. First, it explains how the Spirit works in the lives of disciples. Second, it aims to clear up the misunderstandings that are rampant today because of false teaching on the Spirit. My earlier book, *The Powerful Delusion* (London, 1987, 1989), focused only on this second aspect. *The Spirit* incorporates about two-thirds of *The Powerful Delusion*, although about one-half of *The Spirit* is "fresh" material.

32. Baptism and the 'Name'

"In Matthew 28:19 Jesus commanded his disciples to baptize the new disciples in the name of the Father and of the Son and of the Holy Spirit. But in Acts 2:38, Peter told us to baptize in the name of Jesus alone. Is there any difference?"

No, I do not believe there is any difference at all. These are simply two ways of saying the same thing. "In the name of" means, essentially, "by the authority of." The Bible never explicitly says there is some verbal formula we must be sure to utter when we perform baptisms. For more on this, see my book *The Spirit.*

33. Baptism by Jesus' Disciples

"John 4:1-2 mentions that Jesus' disciples were baptizing, but Jesus had not yet died and been resurrected. So, were they applying a form of the baptism of John? Did those disciples of John who had presumably previously been baptized by him (like Andrew) need to be baptized again?"

Yes, I understand the passage to refer to the baptism of John—the pre-Pentecostal baptism. From Pentecost on, things were different. As for whether the disciples of John needed a second baptism, this is very hard to prove from the Bible. While it is possible that Apollos was immersed by Aquila, Acts 18:24ff never says that he was. In contrast, the Ephesian disciples of John's movement, who presumably received John's baptism some time after the new covenant was already in effect, were indeed baptized by Paul. The apostles themselves are not recorded as being immersed again at Pentecost. Jesus in fact described them as "clean" (John 13 and 15) because of the Word he had spoken to them (John 8). They were apparently saved before the day of Pentecost. For more discussion of this question, see my book *The Spirit.*

34. Polygamy

"Are there disciples in Africa who are married to more than one person, and if so, how is that Biblical?"

Yes, I once shared a taxi ride with a disciple in one of our African churches. We began to talk about his family, and it became apparent quite quickly that he had a tangled family situation. I asked him, "Do you have two wives?" While I had heard of this happening, especially in the Muslim regions of the world, I must admit it felt odd to be sitting with a bigamist who was also a disciple. The important point is that polygamy is legal or illegal according to the national law. The Bible teaches the following about polygamy:

- While common in the Old Testament, it never facilitated a happy home life (e.g. Genesis 29-31).
- While rare in the New Testament, it disqualified a man from serving as an elder (e.g. 1 Timothy 3).
- We must obey the laws of the land. In many nations polygamy is against the law and thus wrong. And yet, since in a few countries it's fully legal, it's not really a Biblical issue in such places. This includes the home nation of the man with whom I shared a taxi.

35. Elders and Marriage

"In a recent Bible study on elders and deacons, I became hung up on a scripture about how an elder must be 'the husband of but one wife....' I wondered what that meant. Did men in the first century commonly have multiple, simultaneous wives? Or was Paul saying, as I suspect, that an elder should not be someone who has been divorced and remarried? I've never heard this aspect of this scripture discussed; usually this scripture is cited simply to show that an elder must be married."

Good observation! From my own study, it seems polygamy was rather rare in the Roman Empire in the first century.

And yet it was not unheard of. Serial marriages, however, were more common among the Romans, as well as among the more liberal Jews, who took Deuteronomy 24 in the loosest possible way. The liberal rabbis said that the "indecent" thing of Deuteronomy 24 might include the wife's burning the dinner or not being sufficiently pretty for the liking of her husband. The more conservative rabbis took the indecency to be adultery or something else that was serious.

You may be right that Paul is saying that men on second or third marriages are disqualified. (If so, I would like to understand exactly *why* that would disqualify them.)

36. Eldership

"I read in Titus 1:6 that a man must have children who believe in order to be considered for eldership. I take this to mean that his children must be old enough to be disciples, yet some men have been appointed as elders in the kingdom whose children are under ten and sometimes under five. What does it mean to have children who believe?"

"Children who believe" is clearly a key concept in this passage. Interpretation of the requirement ranges between *all one's children being Christians* and *at least one* being a disciple. (Important note: In the International Churches of Christ, no one has been appointed who did not have at least one child who had made the adult decision to become a disciple.)

"Children who believe" is equivalent to "children who are true Christians" (having repented and been baptized). It isn't referring to belief in general. The Bible does not specify explicitly whether every child need be a disciple (yet). It also does not discuss the implications of a child leaving the Lord later in life or other possible exceptions or mitigating circumstances. The fundamental point seems obvious, though: The elder must be excellent at building family.

37. After Death

"If our final destination is determined upon reaching Hades, why would salvation judgment not occur immediately following physical death? Why should it take place when Christ returns? When does the 'works' judgment occur, as is implied in 2 Corinthians 5:10, Matthew 16:27, etc.?"

Although "salvation judgment" is not a specifically Biblical phrase, let us use it as a working term. I am not so sure salvation judgment *doesn't* take place at the point of death. Your destiny is, for all intents and purposes, fixed once you die. (There's no purgatory, no commutation of sentence!) That's why I think reward/punishment begins at that time.

Once Jesus returns, we are resurrected and stand before the judgment bar of God. This judgment is, I believe, *declarative*, not *investigative*. In other words, the Lord is not carrying on some sort of *investigation* to determine whether we lived righteously enough to make it to heaven. Rather, he will *declare* what we already know to be the case.

Yesterday I read 2 Corinthians, came across 5:10 (which you mention in your question) and pondered the situation further. Since Christians are saved through Christ, could it not be that when we appear before the judgment bar of Christ, the Lord will, in some sense, review our lives and let us know about our "treasure in heaven"—a doctrine Jesus himself taught? If the notion of degrees of reward in heaven makes you at all uncomfortable, consider whether it isn't usually the case that the more you put into something, the more you get out of it? If you work hard with your sports team to achieve a victory, the victory is even sweeter than if you only gave eighty percent. There is thus a little extra reward for those who truly went the distance. Does this make sense?

Of course while Christians are to live a God-fearing life, we are not to live in dread of damnation, unsure of whether we have measured up.[4]

If you would like more information, please see the appendix in my book *The God Who Dared*, which is entitled "Another Day in Paradise: What Happens When We Die?" To be frank, this is a position I resisted for nearly twenty years, and yet from my study of the Scriptures, I see no other way to make sense of all the Biblical evidence. Study it out, and have fun!

38. When We Die

"In some scriptures it appears that we are judged immediately at death (Luke 16:23), while in other scriptures it appears that we are all brought together for a final judgment (Matthew 25:31-32). Which is it, or is it both?"

"I want to hear your insights regarding what happens when we die. I've studied out the topic some on my own and have gathered that we enter a state of 'rest' or 'sleep' when we die and then are 'awakened' on Judgment Day. I've often heard people say that when true Christians die, they are 'with God,' but it would seem the answer is 'not yet.' What light can you shed on this topic?"

It feels like hundreds of disciples are asking about what happens after death. I wrestled with these questions for a number of years, resisting the view to which I have now come. (All of us must do our best to interpret the Scriptures in a way that makes sense to us; this may involve a prolonged period of time, during which our views may go back and forth.) I finally published my view in 1997 in *The God Who Dared,* Appendix E. Let me summarize, however, how I understand the sequence of events:

Death $\rightarrow$ Hades $\rightarrow$ Second Coming $\rightarrow$ Resurrection $\rightarrow$ Final Judgment $\rightarrow$ Heaven/Hell

After we live, we die (once, no reincarnation—Hebrews 9). If we die lost, we don't need to wait until Judgment Day to find out where we stand. John 3:18 says that those who do not believe already stand condemned; 2 Peter 2 speaks of punishment *before* Judgment Day, yet after death. Yet for the redeemed, there is something awesome that happens after death. Like the penitent thief, we go to paradise—not heaven. Jesus insisted that no one had gone into heaven except the one who came from heaven (John 3:13). Peter said that not even David ascended to heaven (Acts 2:34). The term "paradise" occasionally refers to heaven, as in Revelation 2, but I believe the picture of the next world that emerges from the Old and New Testaments forces us to distinguish paradise from heaven.

One important reason I think that no one has ever gone to heaven is that Jesus taught that this was dependent on his coming again (John 14). He said he was going there to prepare a place for us. One day he will return to take us there; yet this return has not taken place yet. John 5 says that when he comes back, all the dead will hear his voice and rise from the dead. So this part of the sequence is Second Coming⟶Resurrection. Yet between death and our resurrection we *are* conscious. Sleep is only a metaphor for death, as in 1 Corinthians 15:51. (The doctrine of "soul sleep" is a false one.) I believe Luke 16 supports this view. Lazarus is in paradise (the metaphor here is "Abraham's bosom"—KJV), while the rich man is in agony. They can see each other. They are in Hades. In older English, "Hades" was rendered "hell"—a very negative word for us, but originally neutral. It was the underworld, with a "good" compartment and a "bad" one as well.

After our resurrection we appear before the judgment seat of Christ. This judgment is declarative, not investigative. God is not trying to figure out whether we are going to be admitted to heaven; he already knows! He's merely declaring officially what our destiny is. The righteous will then (not before) go to heaven. The lost will be cast into the lake of fire, which is the "second death."[5] So where are disciples who have died? They are in paradise; they are conscious and they are happy. And yet, I don't think it is correct to state that they are in heaven: not yet, not until the Lord returns.

39. Fasting

"I have a question about fasting. I have never read the *Didache*, but I believe it contains information that deals with fasting. In the first century church, did Christians fast twice a week on days different from Jewish practice? If so, why don't we fast twice a week? Also, why do Catholics fast during Lent and (sometimes) during Advent? Why do they not eat meat on Fridays?"

The *Didache,* an early Christian work that speaks of the practice of fasting (among other things), does indeed record the practice you mention. And yet, as this is not commanded in the Bible, we are under no obligation at all to follow it. Even if the apostles did follow such a practice, the Spirit of Christ did not lead them to instruct us to do the same (John 14:26, 16:13).

The Catholic practice of a Wednesday and Friday fast—common by around the third century—was eventually commuted to abstinence from meat only (fish was an exception) on one day a week. Again, I do not believe that there is any Biblical authority in the Catholic practice that would require us to institute regular fast days. Yes, the church did become rather fond of fasting (as in the Lenten period). Yet in time they also became fond of calling men "father," forbidding marriage, worshiping relics and worshiping Mary as the "mother of God" and the "Queen of Heaven."

It really boils down to the question of authority. Disciples believe the only binding authority in our lives is *Biblical* authority.

40. Christ Dies Today?

"Christ died on the cross two thousand years ago. How does he die for me now, when it happened two thousand years ago?"

To be theologically correct, Christ doesn't die for us today. The Bible teaches that he died "once for all." (Check this phrase in the book of Hebrews with your concordance; there are several references.) We may occasionally *imagine* Christ on the cross, as in our prayers during the Lord's Supper. Yet Jesus' death is past; now he reigns in heaven and intercedes for us.

41. Dual Prophecy

"Can you explain twofold prophecy? In Daniel, Isaiah, Matthew 24 and Revelation, for example, there are prophecies already fulfilled, yet some people say they also point to future events. How do you know which prophecies are twofold?"

Let me refer you to the units in *The Bible on Trial* column that deal with prophecy. For a short answer, however, here are a few pointers:

- Each prophecy must be studied in context.
- The historical background of the book must be understood.
- Any secondary fulfillment must be demanded by the text or explicitly indicated in the New Testament.
- Nearly all of what you read today in Christian literature or hear on Christian radio concerning prophecy is nonsense.

Fee and Stuart's *How to Read the Bible for All Its Worth* would be a great book to study—especially the section on prophetic literature.

42. Matthew = Levi?

"In Matthew 9:9 the Bible says that Jesus called Matthew, a tax collector, whereas in Mark 2:14 the Bible says that Jesus called Levi, the son of Alphaeus. My confusion is over why there is a name difference. Are they the same person?"

You are right: Levi and Matthew are one and the same. It was quite common for a Jew to have both a Hebrew name (Levi) and a Greek/Roman one (Matthew).[6]

43. Clarification on Gospel Harmony

"I am concerned about an encouragement you gave in an e-mail: 'I would encourage you not to use words of Jesus from one section of one gospel to illuminate the meaning of other words of his in another section of an entirely different gospel.' You were discussing Luke 14 at the time. I have loved reading harmonies of the Gospels for years—to me these works 'flesh out' different events in Jesus' life. In light of your encouragement, what attitude should I have as to a 'harmony'? Anyway, are not all the writings works of the Holy Spirit? Why should I beware of turning from one gospel to another for clarification or for deeper study of either an event in Jesus' life or one of his studies—such as the events surrounding the cross or Jesus' Sermon on the Mount? (Matthew 5-7, cross-referencing Luke 6)."

Thank you for your question. It certainly is appropriate many times to compare one gospel to another in order to "flesh out" an event. Though I seem to have misled some of my readers, I was merely trying to suggest that we study each book in its own right before jumping to another book for clarification (as in the case of Luke 14 and Matthew 10). When we are dealing with narratives, fleshing out will at times be more necessary. When we are studying doctrine, it is best at the outset to contain our search: same writer, same book and even same passage if possible. The further afield we search, the less likely contextually the "answer" we find will truly relate to the original question. Moreover, each gospel has its own viewpoint, its own theology. The Spirit is showing us different things; overharmonizing can obliterate the differences. Like putting all your vegetables in a blender, the meal (though it all goes to the same place, your stomach) loses something in being "homogenized."

44. The Use of 'Lord' and 'God' in the New Testament

"You said in your article 'The Trinity' that the Father is God, the Son is God, and the Spirit is God—but that the Father is not the Son, the Son is not the Spirit, and the Spirit is not the Father. Yet 2 Corinthians 3:17-18 says that 'the Lord is the Spirit.' Can you please explain this to me, because it seems that 'the Lord' is most often used in the New Testament to refer to Jesus (except in cases where the Old Testament is quoted)."

Before I begin, I am wondering if you have consulted any commentaries on 2 Corinthians. (Men with better minds than mine have tackled these kinds of questions, and their work is on public record.)

You are right that "Lord" in the New Testament most often refers to Jesus, the second person of the trinity. In the Old Testament, "Lord" refers to the Father or to the whole Godhead. In fact, all three persons of the trinity are "Lord" in the same sense that all are "God." The exact sense needs to be determined by the specific context.

45. Mark 11:24

"In converting people, where is the line drawn between your own faith for them (believing they will become disciples) and their own personal decisions? I have been told that if I believe someone will make the decision to be a disciple, it will happen. On the other hand, the Scriptures are clear that we must all change personally by our own free will. We decide to surrender. The Scriptures seem to teach both. I need to make sure I have the correct viewpoint and that I teach the correct viewpoint to those I lead."

I appreciate your insistence on holding to sound theology, because the notion you discuss in your question is as false as it is common. Broadly speaking, such thinking is called "word-faith" theology. In short, if you believe it (or "claim" it), it will happen. This wrongheaded thinking is based on a misunderstanding of Mark 11:24 and other passages. In essence, if we can only convince ourselves that God will answer our prayers, he will; thus, we control God.

This view is first cousin to the eastern "mind over matter" teaching. And yet by sheer willpower we can create nothing! Our prayers must be in accordance with God's will, as 1 John 5:14-15 teaches. The view is second cousin to "prosperity theology," which is so easily justified by the attitude that says: "Whatever I want I can manage to get, if I want it badly enough."

Thank you for noticing this error. Please speak up if ever you hear it propagated again. Our prayers can never obliterate others' free will—though by God's power minds can be changed (as happened in the case of your own conversion and mine).

46. Self-Defense

"Jesus teaches us to love our enemies. Does this mean that if a person attacks me—or for that matter, tries to attack my wife or my child—I should remain silent and watch him? Can I hit him back in self-defense? If yes, and if we are involved in a scuffle in which the attacker loses his life, would I be guilty of committing murder?"

Jesus teaches that we should be people of love. I believe most of my readers would agree that to sit back and do nothing while an attacker was threatening my family would *not* be loving. In other words, there is a higher principle at work here. (I for one would certainly protect my family!)

Interestingly, though we have to be very careful in applying OT teachings to our NT situations, the Law may shed a little light on the subject. Exodus 22:2-3a reads, "If a thief is caught breaking in and is struck so that he dies, the defender is not guilty of bloodshed; but if it happens after sunrise, he is guilty of bloodshed." In some sense, it would

appear that the violence done to the burglar was "necessary." I wish I could give you more help here. It is obviously a complex issue, and I prefer not to be dogmatic.

47. Joseph of Arimathea = Jesus' Uncle?

"I came across the public television show, "Mysteries of the
Bible" (talking about Jesus' crucifixion and resurrection).
They made mention of a theory that Joseph of Arimathea
was Jesus' uncle. According to this theory, Jesus had most
likely accompanied him into the northern regions as a young
boy on his 'business trips' to trade goods. They were inti-
mating that this is the main reason why Joseph was concerned with burying Jesus (his beloved nephew), not so
much that he believed Jesus was the Christ. What is your
view of this theory?"

Though I have come across the view that Joseph was one of
the men who brought the faith to England, I have never
come across this view, which sounds even more speculative. Whatever Joseph's motivation for interring Jesus' body,
our view on this matter has no doctrinal implications.

48. Tithing

"I was always taught to tithe and have always done so, and
God has blessed my family tremendously. Yet the evangelist in my new ministry situation does not believe in pressing the issue of giving ten percent with his people. He says
the New Testament says nothing about a tithe, so he doesn't
feel right pressing the issue. Will this be something we just
disagree on?"

Personally, I agree with your evangelist. The New Testament nowhere teaches a mandatory tithe. There is in fact no
minimum level of giving acceptable to the Lord—and no
maximum level, either. It will depend totally on the
individual's situation. However—and this is a *big* "however"—

in the First World, there are very, very few of us who can't give *well over ten percent* if we are prioritizing the kingdom in our lives and not simply spending our money as the rest of the world does. The Bible has much to say about money—more than we tend to be comfortable with.

As you study the Bible with prospective disciples, it is important to cover issues such as stewardship and material-ism (Ephesians 5:3-5). Jesus himself taught many parables on our attitudes toward and use of wealth (see especially the gospel of Luke). I would encourage you to do your own study; hopefully, this will not be an area in which you will have to "agree to disagree."

49. 1 Corinthians 7:12 and Inspiration

"I have a question regarding scriptures that seem to imply that they are not God-breathed, for instance, 'To the rest I say this (I, not the Lord)'—1 Corinthians 7:12. Is this God-breathed?"

1 Corinthians 7 is basically a commentary on Matthew 19. In Matthew, Jesus lays down the law for marriage between two covenant people. Jesus did not teach about the situa-tion between a believer and a nonbelieving spouse. That was for the Spirit to accomplish through Paul.

"I, not the Lord" does not mean Paul doubts his inspira-tion (just see the final verse of 1 Corinthians 7). It means, in effect, "I am speaking about an issue the Lord did not cover." Similarly, "Not I, but the Lord" is not meant to distinguish between levels of inspiration or authority, but simply to remind the reader that on covenant marriages the Lord had already spoken.

50. 2 Timothy 3:16

"Is 2 Timothy 3:16-17 speaking of the Old Testament when it says, 'All Scripture'? The entire Bible as we know it wasn't even completed at that point, right? So is it logical for us to say from this passage that Scripture states that all of the Bible comes from God?"

You are right that the passage in question discusses the Old Testament, to which Paul had been referring to in verses 14 and 15. You are also right that most of the New Testament had not been written by the time of 2 Timothy (67-68 AD or so). To apply this passage to the New Testament requires an extension of the principle, and this may not be obvious to everyone.

There are actually many lines of reasoning we can follow to understand why the whole Bible comes from God. (See the archived material on the Aces Online.) As for 2 Timothy 3, when I teach from this passage, I usually comment that in context it refers to the Old Testament. Yet I also mention that 1 Timothy 5 quotes from the gospel of Luke as "Scripture." I remind people that Jesus himself promised in John 14:26 and 16:13 that there was more Scripture to come—after his departure—and it would come through the apostolic ministry. As you know, the apostles and their immediate disciples wrote the entire New Testament.

51. The Transfiguration

"My question is on Matthew 17, the transfiguration of Jesus. First, what is the purpose for this story? What am I supposed to learn from it? Second, why did God choose Elijah and Moses, and whom do they represent? Third, who is Elijah in this story, the OT Elijah?"

The account of the transfiguration shows us that the ministry of Jesus (the gospel) is complementary to, yet also superior to, the ministries of Moses (the Law) and Elijah (the Prophets). Yes, this is the same Elijah who appears in the Old Testament and in whose spirit John the Baptist prepared the way for the Lord.

52. The Heavenly Realms

"What is the meaning of Ephesians 3:10? Don't those in the heavenly realms already know the manifold wisdom of God? They can see God, or rather they see the spiritual realms (and we can't), so don't they already know about God? What do you think the passage means?"

Let me quote here from a soon-to-be-published work on Ephesians—*God's Perfect Plan for Imperfect People* by Thomas Jones (to be released by DPI in February 2001):

> The expression "the heavenly realms" appears in Ephesians 1:20, 2:6, 3:10 and 6:12. It is not a synonym for heaven, but rather a reference to the realm of the spirit. God is there (in the first three references), but the rulers and powers of darkness are also found there (the latter two references). The spiritual battles are ultimately fought in the "heavenly realms"—those realms that are not a part of space/time universe. In 3:20 we see that the powers of darkness have the manifold wisdom of God held up to them as they see Jews and Gentiles coming together in one body. All their efforts are designed to divide, embitter and alienate, but the gospel declares to them that God through the cross has found the way to defeat them in their evil schemes.

53. Taking Up the Cross

"When the Bible says 'take up his cross daily' (Luke 9:23), what does that really mean—to kill your sin or to bear Jesus' persecution? To me, 'deny himself' and 'take up his cross daily' are almost interchangeable."

Yes, the concepts are very similar. By the cross we crucify our flesh (Romans 6:6, Colossians 3:5), yet crucifixion is also a metaphor for our radically new lives (dead to the old self)—Galatians 2:20, 5:24, 6:14.

I believe the image of someone carrying his own cross was a shocking one in the first century, when public executions by crucifixion left an indelible imprint in the minds of men, women and probably even children. So, does Jesus mean we will die *literally*? Perhaps, though not likely, with the added adverb "daily." If you ever hear someone say that believing in Jesus in the first century would have been easy, all you have to do is point him or her to this teaching that would have been shocking and radical to all who heard it. This would have been true however you interpreted it.

54. The Rapture

"What is 'The Rapture,' and what scriptural references do proponents of this idea use as supporting evidence? I fail to get a clear understanding from the often quoted 1 Thessalonians 4:13-5:11. Also, what is to become of the unsaved 'left behind' after this supposed event?"

The popular rapture doctrine comes from 1 Thessalonians 4 and the book of Revelation, awkwardly forced together so that the righteous are beamed up to heaven, while the wicked remain behind on earth, suffering God's outpoured wrath. No, this doctrine just will not do! In John 5, Jesus says that, on his return, everybody will be resurrected, good and wicked alike, to face judgment. Revelation, in context, though it provides timeless lessons on God's faithfulness and stern treatment of the church's persecutors, describes punishment to fall on the Roman Empire, not some supposed twenty-first century cataclysm. The *Left Behind* series, I am sure, is bringing in a fortune to its writers—too bad it isn't based on sound doctrine.

The Bible teaches that when Christ returns, those *who are still alive* (1 Thessalonians 4) will rise to meet Christ in the air or be "raptured." But 1 Thessalonians nowhere says that everyone else will be left behind to face punishment. Quite simply, the punishment of Hades and hell are not of this world.[7]

55. The Book of Job

"I think Job is such an inspiring book, but I must admit that reading it makes me feel a little insecure. Oftentimes, the words of the 'worthless physicians' (Job 13) or 'miserable comforters' (Job 16) seem rather wise and spiritual to me. Yet obviously God doesn't think their words are worthy of esteem (Job 42:7). Can you offer some insight on how to view and interpret this incredible book?"

There are a number of speakers in the book of Job. While this book comes to us by the inspiration of God, this does not mean that every speaker is telling the truth! Consider these characters in the book:

- God—his words are pure and faultless.
- Job—his words, despite their occasional bad attitude, are on the whole on target.
- Job's wife—her words hardly make for a wholesome philosophy of life.
- Elihu—unlike the "miserable comforters," he is not rebuked by God, for he does not espouse popular theology.
- Eliphaz, Bildad and Zophar—you are right, the "worthless physicians" are spouting off nonsense, and God himself upbraids them for teaching error, although truth is often mixed with their errors.

I would strongly recommend that you carefully read Fee and Stuart's *How to Read the Bible for All Its Worth.* They have an excellent section on how to read the Wisdom Literature, the literary genre to which Job belongs.

Short answer: Be extremely wary of quoting from the book of Job. Chances are, the "wisdom" you are tapping into is conventional and incorrect. Be sure you consider the context and the speaker before you frame a quote and put it on your wall.

56. The Tetragrammaton

"The Jehovah's Witnesses claim that the name of God, Jehovah, was taken out of the Scriptures. It was my understanding that the tetragrammaton (YHWH) was too holy to pronounce and that to this day the Jews do not use it for the name of

God. Is this true? If this is the Father's preferred name and the simple name 'God' is too vague, I want to know."

It is true that the Jews are loathe to pronounce God's covenant name, *Yahweh*. Even in writing, it is not uncommon to see the word "God" shortened to "G-d."

The "tetragrammaton" (from the Greek for "four-lettered [word]") refers to the four consonants that make up the word for "God" in the Hebrew Old Testament. They are Y-H-W-H. Truth is, no one can say for sure how this was pronounced, since the text lacks vowels. Without the vocalization, we can only guess. Scholars today posit that the original pronunciation was *Yahweh*. The tetragrammaton derives from the Hebrew verb "to be," and refers to God's existence, which is eternal and self-sustained. There are special echoes of the Name in the gospel of John, where over and over Jesus says, "I am…" ("the bread of life," "the resurrection and the life," "the gate," etc.). In John 8:58 the Lord says, "…before Abraham was born, I am!" This was considered blasphemous because it was a direct claim to divinity.

At any rate, "Jehovah" is a total mispronunciation of the Hebrew, so the Jehovah's Witnesses are being quite inconsistent when they insist on a particular pronunciation for God's name and then fail to get it right.

57. The 'Lost Tribes'

"I have become curious about the 'lost tribes' of Israel and the connection with Europe, Britain and the US inferred by some groups. What do they base this idea on, and what are your thoughts on the issue? If the viewpoint is a distorted one (my current presumption), what is the motivation for the misinterpretation?"

Well, I cannot speak on the motivation that drives people to speculate about the lost tribes—maybe it's a desire to support racial supremacy of one kind or another, which is a common motive in religion. The Scriptures teach that the tribe of Judah (along with Benjamin and Levi) remained true to the Lord for many years, while all the others strayed. The lost tribes were not lost to the New World or to the western limit of the Old World. They were lost through intermarriage. (See 2 Kings 17.) This was in the eighth century BC.

58. Matthew 11:13

"What do you think Matthew 11:13 means? If all the Prophets and the Law prophesied until John, why is the revelation in the Bible?"

I was reading this very passage the morning I received your e-mail! Revelation from God continued until the New Testament was completed, most likely somewhere between 69 and 96 AD. John is usually recognized as the last of the old covenant prophets, strictly speaking. Jesus, in this passage, is accentuating the fact that with his message, something new is happening; and the Old Testament (Law and Prophets) point and lead to Christ and his message. Here is a nutshell picture of Biblical revelation, with approximate dates:

1400 BC......... 750-450 BC............. 30 AD .... 40-70 AD
Law .... Prophets .... John .... New
                                                    Testament

59. Other Sheep

"While discussing the Bible with a friend from a Mormon background, the topic of the 'other sheep' of John 10 came up. The Mormons use this scripture to contend that Jesus visited 'Christians' on the continent of North America. I'm not sure what it means and do not know how to refute this belief within the context of the scripture. What 'other sheep' could Jesus be referring to? Since he was directly addressing a Jewish audience in John 10, was he referring to the Gentiles or other uncircumcised peoples who would be reached through Paul?"

Yes indeed, the "other sheep" are the Gentiles. The mystery of the gospel was that the Gentiles would ultimately be blessed along with the Jews (from Genesis 12:3 on; see also Ephesians 3:8-11). The Mormons came up with their peculiar view in the nineteenth century, as they struggled to distinguish themselves from other groups. At the time they also taught that the moon and sun were inhabited! Some zany beliefs have been retracted or expunged from their literature; others have remained.

60. Parable of the Weeds

"I always had the understanding (or misunderstanding) that on the day Jesus returns, disciples will be taken up into heaven first. However, Matthew 13:30 (the Parable of the Weeds) reads, 'Let both grow together until the harvest. At that time I will tell the harvesters: First collect the weeds and tie them in bundles to be burned; then gather the wheat and bring it into my barn.' Could you please shed some light on the subject?"

As for disciples being taken up into heaven, 1 Thessalonians 4 indicates the disciples who are living at the time of Jesus' return will be taken up, not all disciples. As for the parable, it is seldom right to press the details of a parable. The image of the harvest seems to represent judgment, and the parable implies that the righteous and the wicked alike will be dealt with at the same time. This is consistent with the day of resurrection to judgment of John 5.

61. Satan's Fate

"Since Satan knows that his fate is sealed, why is he acting as he does? Is he betting that God's love will eventually lead to a reprieve? Or is Satan just wanting to hurt God by showing him how many of his beloved creatures will follow him into the pit instead of listening to the Father?"

You are asking me to speculate here. (So I will!) I doubt that Satan is banking on any sort of reprieve. No, it seems to me he is simply unwilling to back down. This is the nature of pride. Like a madman holed up in a battle with the police, he knows his ultimate destiny but just wants to take as many people out as possible.

62. Destroy Satan?

"Since Satan always tempts people to do wicked things, why does God not destroy Satan? Also, did God know that Adam and Eve would eat from the tree of the knowledge of good and evil? If not, does it mean God was not powerful enough to control it?"

First, God's way is to prove that his system is better than Satan's. While he could certainly settle everything in a split second—as Jesus could have called ten thousand angels (Matthew 26:53)—the Lord's way is to support those who, by their own free will, choose to follow him.

Second, God certainly knew what the first couple would do, and the Scriptures affirm that the sacrifice of Jesus Christ was anticipated, and in fact prepared, before the foundation of the world (1 Peter 1:20).

Third, if by "control," you mean "prevent," it should be quickly said that the Lord is most able to prevent *all* of our sin. But would we still be human then? He could have created a race of automatons, but the essence of personality is free will. And even though the Lord knows that only a minority of his creatures will accept his sovereignty and Lordship—most will be lost—this is evidently better than the alternative of removing the capacity for wrong choices. Otherwise, God would have created that kind of a world.

63. Reuel

"I have a question about Exodus 2:16-3:1. When reading this section, it appears that Reuel is Moses' father-in-law and not Jethro. Who is Reuel?"

Reuel is simply another name for Jethro. Back then, as now, it happened sometimes that a person had more than one name.

64. John's Baptism Vs. Baptism in Jesus' Name

"In John 3:22 and John 4:2, the Bible says that the disciples of Jesus were baptizing. What kind of baptism was this? In Romans 6:1-7, the Scriptures say Jesus had to die, be buried and then be resurrected in order for baptism to take effect. If it was John's baptism, then why were Jesus' disciples following John's teaching when Jesus was there with them?"

John's baptism prepared the people for the coming of the Lord, as Malachi 3 and 4 prophesied, and as in fact John's ministry did through insisting that people be reconciled to one another *before* they went under the water. In addition, the association between water and forgiveness, already present in the Old Testament (Leviticus 14, Numbers 19, etc.) was greatly strengthened. The short answer to your question: John's baptism brought people near to God; their sins were forgiven (Mark 1:4).

A few facts about John's baptism:

- It brought forgiveness of sins (Mark 1:4).
- It did not confer the Spirit (John 7:39).
- It in no way connected to those baptized into Christ (Romans 6), since the key events of the gospel had not yet taken place (death, burial, resurrection—see 1 Corinthians 15:3-4).
- Thus the baptism administered by Jesus' disciples was *not* baptism in Jesus' name (Acts 2:38), but something different which we call "John's baptism."
- Finally, it is true that the nucleus of Jesus' original movement came from the ranks of John. John's movement and Jesus' movement, at least before Jesus' death, were not mutually exclusive. (See Acts 19:1-6 for an illustration of how this would change once the church of Christ had been established.)

65. John's Baptism

"In Acts 19:1-7 the men Paul spoke to were disciples. Where were those men standing with God if they had repented and been baptized and forgiven of their sins? What 'Holy Spirit' was Paul talking about then, and what difference did it make in their relationship with God?"

Yes, Acts 19 mentions "disciples." But does "disciples" in this passage mean they were saved? The term "disciple" sometimes stands as a synonym for a Christian, though more often it connotes the commitment, or learner's stance, of the individual. Another question: is this section meant to stand as a *parallel* to the case of Apollos (18:24ff) or as a *contrast?* There are two possible understandings and which you choose will influence your answers to all the questions that are involved.

They had been baptized with John's baptism, which evidently some branch of his movement, or combination of it with Jesus' movement, still retained. But to equate repentance, baptism and forgiveness of sins under John's ministry with the corresponding elements in the new covenant is not theologically sound. We are comparing apples to oranges. Another question might be, "Were these men baptized with John's baptism *after* it had run its course, or *before?*" It appears they could have known of the Spirit, and should have, but their hybrid theology was a result of an outmoded system being followed after its "expiration date."

The Spirit here is either an external outpouring (as in Acts 8 and 10) or possibly the reception of the indwelling, though I am not convinced that this is what Luke is trying to show us. As you know, without the Spirit (indwelling), we do not belong to Christ (Romans 8:9). Although I would like to be more decisive here, I admit the interpretation of this passage may need to remain a "gray area." For more thoughts, see my book *The Spirit.*

66. Tithing on Nonsalary Income

"I have been studying out the difference or lack of difference between tithing from my firstfruits (I equate this with my income) and honoring God with my wealth (created by growth in my home equity, investments, retirement accounts and the like). My practice is to give proportionally, based on my year to year income growth. I'm eager to understand if differences exist between 'firstfruits' and 'wealth,' Biblically speaking."

You may well equate "firstfruits" with your income, but what exegetical reason do you have to insist that this is valid? Firstfruits have to do with agriculture, as does the entire tithing system. I will assume you do not want an in-depth discussion of the tithing issue, so let me address the matter of whether the disciple is obliged to give back to the church some part of his nonsalary income (the types of income you mention).

Legalistic answer: You should give one and one-half percent on your extra income if it is an inheritance (based on an application of Numbers 31:28-30[8]), ten percent on other income, but nothing on retirement accounts (since you will presumably tithe anyway once you withdraw your money).

What I really think: This is totally up to you. Do what you feel God wants you to do. Do it cheerfully, not under compulsion.

67. Who's Reporting?

"When the New Testament talks about what happens and explains peoples' hearts and motives behind their actions, is it because a disciple was there with them? For example, Matthew 27:1-10—who is reporting these facts?"

Sometimes eyewitness reports were relied upon (2 Peter 1:16), sometimes written sources (see the prologue to Luke). Sometimes God even revealed things that no one else could have known or remembered (John 14:26, 16:13). Matthew 27 is an easier passage, because there would have been scores of witnesses. Usually, with a little bit of creativity, it is not hard to imagine how the writers knew the things they knew. Of course, it is always also possible that God moved them in a special way, endowing them with knowledge entirely beyond them.

68. Miscellaneous Questions from Genesis 1-11

"Were Adam and Eve the only humans God personally, directly created? Cain went out and got a wife. Later he built a city, etc. Where did these people come from? How long were Adam and Eve in the Garden? If Adam named all the animals, was he around when there were dinosaurs?"

"What about the two creation accounts in Genesis? It is not that there are two accounts that bothers me, but the sequence of events seems to differ. In Genesis 2, creation went from streams right to man, unlike the first chapter's account—although it does say that God 'had' planted the garden (v8) and that he 'had' formed the animals (v19). Is there anything you know that would clear this up?"

Genesis 1-11 is one of the Bible's main hotbeds, generating question after question. (The other hot spot is Revelation.) Interesting, isn't it? The opening and the closing of the Bible, which touch on primeval and eternal time, speak to us in a different way than the rest of the Bible (everything in the middle). There are 1,100 chapters in the Bible, and I am amazed by how many questions come from the first eleven chapters of Genesis. My own interest was sparked when I was sixteen years old, and I have not stopped reading on the subject since then.

If you don't mind, this time I would like to refer you also to my book on Genesis, *The God Who Dared*. Every question you posed is dealt with there. I find these kinds of questions truly fascinating, and I would encourage you to read as much as you need to so that your questions are answered. At the end of my book, I provide some biblio-graphical suggestions that will help you even more. Some-times when I travel, I conduct presentations on Genesis. Worldwide, audiences always ask lots of good questions. You can tell, I usually prefer to point people to sources where they can find the answers, rather than just giving them "the answer" myself. After all, we need to have our own convictions based on what we have studied and expe-rienced, not on authority or someone else's opinion.

Whatever you, the reader, think about these things, be sure that these are not matters of salvation. I recall sharing my faith on the streets of London and meeting some very religious chaps whose entire church was based around the "correct" interpretation of Genesis. I followed them to an informal church service, and as soon as they realized I didn't necessarily agree with their view, I was hauled over the coals. The entire church group dedicated the next two hours of its meeting to me. While I did not think they were saved because the Spirit of Christ and discipleship were lacking, they were adamant that I was not saved because I didn't subscribe to their view that the earth is only a few thousand years old! Since proper understanding of these issues is not essential to salvation, make sure that you keep a spirit of grace and openness to others who may see things differ-ently (a word to the wise).

Notes

[1] For more on Josephus, you might like to see my chapters on the life and letter of James in *Life to the Full*, 20-48.

[2] Anthony A. Hoekema, *Seventh Day Adventism* (Grand Rapids: Wm. B. Eerdmans, 1973).

[3] John Driver, *How Christians Made Peace with War* (Scottsdale, Penn.: Herald Press, 1988).

[4] For more on this, see Gordon Ferguson's excellent book *The Victory of Surrender—Second Edition*. See also my response to question 11b in *The Bible on Trial*.

[5] For more on this, see the essay on hell in the last section of this book and see *The Bible on Trial*, question 50b.

[6] For more on this, may I recommend William S. McBirnie's *The Search for the Twelve Apostles* (Wheaton: Tyndale, 1976). The book is somewhat out of date and speculative, but contains many accounts of the lives, names, travels and impact of all the apostles (even Thomas' work in South India).

[7] For much more information see *The Final Act* by Steve Kinnard (Woburn, Mass.: DPI, 2000).

[8] Here spoils of war are assessed. Two percent is to go to the Levites (not the usual ten percent), and surprisingly only one-fifth percent to the Lord! That makes a total of two and two-tenths percent. So we see the ten percent rule is waived in a case of "income" over and above the normal level. How does this fit with our teaching on tithing? Certainly we must admit that the tithe is not an *absolute* rule on all income.

4
Various and Sundry

1. LXX

"In your online column you wrote '... remember that often when the New Testament quotes the Old Testament, it is making use of the "LXX,"' but what is the LXX?"

In Roman numerals, I = 1, V = 5, X = 10, L = 50, C = 100, M = 1000, D = 5000, etc. The symbol LXX, Roman numerals for "70," refers to the ancient Greek translation of the Bible by the Jews. LXX in Latin is *septuaginta;* hence it is written "LXX," but read "Septuagint." Tradition held that seventy translators compiled this translation of the Old Testament—which is approximately ninety-seven percent Hebrew, three percent Aramaic—into Greek. The translation was completed a couple of centuries before Christ.

A note for our linguists or Greek readers: it is possible to purchase the Septuagint, with or without English translation. Christians affirm that the *original* Hebrew books of the Bible are inspired.

2. Islam

"What evidence proves the falseness of the Muslim faith?"

Rather than aim to demonstrate the error of other religions, denominations or sects, Christians are called to proclaim the truth and to let their lights shine. The positive focus will draw others to Christ much more than a negative demonstration of the ignorance and lostness of those who do not know God. Still, there is an important place in faith-building apologetics for studying other systems of beliefs.

Since your question is about Islam, let me make a couple of recommendations. First, read the Qur'an. It is only four-fifths of the length of the New Testament, and this will help you to understand the Muslim faith. (I would probably not aim to read the Qur'an if you have not completely read the Bible at least once or twice; keep those priorities straight!) As you read the Qur'an, you'll easily notice the confusion when it comes to OT and NT events.

Second, I recommend the best book I have ever read on Islam, Norman Geisler's and Abdul Saleeb's *Answering Islam: The Crescent in the Light of the Cross* (Grand Rapids: Baker, 1993).

Bringing a Muslim to Christ involves more than knowledge alone. Friendship is needed! Fundamentally, the Muslim is no different than you or me. He is a sinner in need of God's forgiveness. Although there is much violence in some Muslim nations, Jesus died for every one of these persons, regardless of their religion. Even Paul, as he relates in 1 Timothy 1, once acted violently toward the disciples. So don't be intimidated!

3. Extra-Biblical History

"Could you suggest some good study material for first century events that are not recorded in the Bible (e.g., the destruction of the Temple and Jerusalem, Paul's execution, Peter's execution, the fire in Rome, etc.)?"

The word for something outside the Bible is "extra-Biblical," from extra (outside) + Biblical. These helpful books will connect you with some great extra-Biblical sources:

- *Ante-Nicene, Nicene and Post-Nicene Fathers [38 vols.]* (Peabody, Massachusetts: Hendrickson, 1995). This is "the works"—probably more than fifteen thousand pages of source material from the late first to the late eighth centuries! It is available in book form or even on CD-ROM.
- Barrett, C.K., *The New Testament Background: Selected Documents* (New York: Harper & Row, 1961).
- Berçot, David, *Will the Real Heretics Please Stand Up: A New Look at Today's Evangelical Church in the Light of Early Christianity* (Tyler, Texas: Scroll, 1989). This is a light and enjoyable read.
- Bruce, F. F., *Jesus & Christian Origins Outside the New Testament* (Toronto: Hodder & Stoughton, 1984). I have found this little book to be invaluable!

- Bruce, F. F., *The Spreading Flame: The Rise and Progress of Christianity from Its First Beginnings to the Conversion of the English* (Carlisle, England: Paternoster, 1958).
- Dowley, Tim., ed., *A Lion Handbook: The History of Christianity* (Grand Rapids: Eerdmans, 1990). This may be difficult to obtain, but it is both compendious and readable.
- Eusebius, *The History of the Church from Christ to Constantine* (New York: Penguin, 1965). Eusebius was Bishop of Caesarea and historian at the court of the Emperor Constantine.
- Green, Michael, *Evangelism in the Early Church* (Grand Rapids: Eerdmans, 1970). Excellent.
- Lightfoot, J. B., [tr.,] *The Apostolic Fathers, Second Edition* (Grand Rapids: Baker, 1989). This is a must!
- Noll, Mark A., *Turning Points: Decisive Moments in the History of Christianity* (Grand Rapids: Baker, 1997). I would recommend this book as well, even though it has relatively little on the earlier period.
- Stevenson, J., ed., *A New Eusebius: Documents Illustrative of the History of the Church to* AD *33* (London: S.P.C.K., 1957).

May God bless us all as we continue to build our libraries! This, of course, requires a positive attitude toward books. I like the sentiment of Erasmus (sixteenth century reformer), who said something to this effect: "Whenever I get money, I buy *books*. If there's anything left over, then I buy food and clothes."

The apostle Paul, too, had a great devotion to his books, even during his final months on earth. He instructed Timothy, "When you come, bring the cloak that I left with Carpus at Troas, and my scrolls [or books], especially the parchments" (2 Timothy 4:13).

4. Archaeology

"Associate Professor Zeev Herzog (Tel Aviv University, Department of Archaeology and Near Eastern Studies) wrote an article in the renowned *Ha'aretz* magazine (October 29, 1999). I would like to know your response to it. In 'Deconstructing the Walls of Jericho,' Herzog states that after seventy years of intensive excavations in the land of Israel, archaeologists have found: The patriarchs' acts are legendary, the Israelites did not sojourn in Egypt or make an exodus, they did not conquer the land. Neither is there any mention of the empire of David and Solomon, nor of the source of belief in the God of Israel."

Archaeology is not always friendly to Biblical studies, though archaeology that is well done does tend to confirm and reinforce the Scriptures. It is interesting that you ask because the night before this was written, I returned from a three-day Biblical archaeology conference in Boston. Some of the scholars' views were so radical (prejudicial) that they accepted little, if anything, from the Scriptures. Others, however, made every effort to harmonize what the word of God says with the physical evidence. It all depends on one's starting place.

Your question is too involved to tackle here. I will comment on just one point and then make a reading suggestion, hoping that the comment and the suggestion will get you started in the right direction.

For years radical archaeologists have claimed that David was a legendary figure, since there is no mention of him outside the Bible. While at the archaeology conference, I attended a lecture on the city of Dan, in the north of Israel. I had the opportunity to visit Dan in September, and it was phenomenal to see the site and hear from the man who has spent more than thirty years excavating it, Avraham Biran. His team made a remarkable find, an Aramean inscription (I believe from the eighth century BC) that mentions the "House of David." Settled! And the examples could be multiplied.

As for the recommendation, there was a surprisingly generous and readable article in *U.S. News and World Report,* October 26, 1999: "Is the Bible True: New discoveries offer surprising support for key moments in the Scriptures." (In fact, it is the cover story.) I would suggest you obtain this and devour it.

5. General and Special Revelation

"How can I help my Hindu friend see the way Christianity builds on top of the foundational truths that most religions share?"

Certain truths are well nigh universal (don't murder or commit adultery, respect your elders, laziness will get you in trouble, etc.) and require no special guidance from God. These truths are "general revelation." Others, however, cannot be known apart from "special revelation"—that which comes in the Judeo-Christian Scriptures and through the life of Jesus Christ. The former have been shown to all men, regardless of religion, which is why they are "without excuse" (see Romans 1:18ff). The latter cannot be known apart from the Bible, which is why sooner or later your friend will need to give his heart to Bible study. I would suggest you read C. S. Lewis' *Mere Christianity,* which does a great job at identifying the common ground across the world religions, while showing the uniqueness of the Christian message.[1]

6. Papacy

"A friend justified the office of the papacy by referring to the office of the 'keybearer' in Isaiah 22:22ff. The keybearer was a successive office that had authority under the king. Now if we allow God to take the equivalent place of the OT king in the New Testament, then a physical head of the church would correspond to the keybearer. Jesus' words to Peter in Matthew 16 use similar wording to the Isaiah passage, only the 'kingdom' reference changes from the kingdom of David to the kingdom of God. I was taken back by his argument and was not able to properly refute it. How should I tackle the issue?"

Very clever argument, though it doesn't *prove* anything. In the Old Testament, God is the real king and the reigning monarch is the physical head. So if there is a NT analog, since God is still the real king, the human office of the papacy would correspond to the king himself, not the keybearer, who was only an underling of the true (human) king. In other words, the interpretation above is completely tendentious. Simple logic suffices in this case.

Yet I am not sure your friend will find this satisfying, since he is probably relying on the authority of his church for the "true" interpretation. I would use Colossians 1:18, Ephesians 1:22-23, Matthew 23:9 and other passages to challenge the notion of the papacy.[2]

Interestingly, Eliakim and Shebna, the royal stewards, are well known to history, not just from Isaiah 22, but from archaeology. The tomb referred to by Isaiah has been located, and the inscription stone is in the Israel Museum in Jerusalem—just to keep your faith on the cutting edge!

7. Faithless Prayers and Changes of Heart

"Can a person's lack of faith prevent someone else from becoming a Christian? And will God—prompted by 'faithful' prayers—change the heart of a person who is not open to obeying his word so that he will repent and turn to him?"

A scary thought and a scary question! Look at it this way: If God automatically saved everyone we failed to reach with the gospel, what would be the point of having us all share our faith? Something very important does depend on us.

I believe it is indeed possible for someone to hurt someone else's chances, whether through low faith, rudeness, harshness or failure to pray sincerely for him. I think this is the sort of thing Jesus had in mind in Matthew 23:13:

> "Woe to you, teachers of the law and Pharisees, you hypocrites! You shut the kingdom of heaven in men's faces. You yourselves do not enter, nor will you let those enter who are trying to."

So it *is* possible to damage someone else's chances. Not that they would not still bear the *primary* responsibility for their choices and for their sins. So, God is just, yet as we see in the New Testament, he *always* works through others to bring us to Christ.

As for the second aspect, whether our prayers can change someone's heart, I believe the answer is yes. Paul in 2 Timothy 2:24-26 says,

> And the Lord's servant must not quarrel; instead, he must be kind to everyone, able to teach, not resentful. Those who oppose him he must gently instruct, in the hope that God will grant them repentance leading them to a knowledge of the truth, and that they will come to their senses and escape from the trap of the devil, who has taken them captive to do his will.

If it is fully within God's power to change the hearts of those that are opposing the truth, then there is hope for anyone.

Your question is a good one and reminds me of the kinds of questions many of our "Sarah's daughters" (those whose husbands do not believe, as in 1 Peter 3) ask. Keep praying, for God is the one who can open the willing heart. We cannot be certain about how this all works. We do know that it is our responsibility to live an exemplary life that makes the message attractive, to pray earnestly for others and then trust God with what results.

8. Predestination

"I know that Jacob and Esau were both Isaac's sons, but God chose Jacob to be one of the ancestors of Jesus. After Jacob, I know that the 'line' went to Judah and so on, as recorded in Matthew 1. It is also said that the roles of Jacob and Esau were predestined before birth. My question is, after Esau and Jacob were born, which of the following is true (unless only God knows)? (1) Jacob's decisions in his life (as well as Esau's and others') could not possibly have changed his role since God had made a choice. That is, Jacob's role was predetermined unconditionally. (2) Jacob's decisions in his life (as well as Esau's and others') could possibly have changed his role since God is a living God, interacting with his people. That is, it is possible that God may change his mind in certain cases."

This is deep stuff! I appreciate your specifying the predestination of Jacob's role as opposed to that of his salvation, since for God to have predestined Jacob to salvation, in addition to its being the misreading of Malachi 1, it would have been patently unfair. I believe that when we keep in mind that God's decisions are based on his foreknowledge, it is easier to accept God's decisions without struggling.

Since God's foreknowledge depends on our free-will choices, it is an academic question whether God's choice could have been different. Since God knows the future (though he does not determine it, being outside our dimension of time), in his wisdom he is able to make choices through which good comes to men and glory is brought to him—choices based squarely on his certainty of how we will choose. In other words, I cannot see how God's omniscience is compatible with any sort of limited knowledge.

I would recommend that you read some of C. S. Lewis's writings, perhaps *The Problem of Pain* or *Miracles,* if you have not already learned to appreciate Lewis' writings. Most confusion about God's sovereign choices and our free will is compounded by failure to appreciate what it means for God to be outside our dimension of time. This is understandable, given the difficulty sometimes of getting our finite minds around these lofty concepts.

To answer your question, I go with neither (1) nor (2). God's choice was based on his advance knowledge of Jacob's choices, so (1) is ruled out. And yet (2) also fails to speak the truth since, as Numbers 23:19 reads, "God is not a man, that he should lie, nor a son of man, that he should change his mind." Even when the Scriptures speak as though God changed his mind, we must always remember that the "change" is change only from our limited, time-bound perspective. God does indeed interact, and his relationship with us is personal, not mechanical. However, his wisdom is infinite and eternal. What we experience, and what is described anthropomorphically for our benefit, never proves a reduction in God's knowledge—no fickleness, no surprises, no change (James 1:17, Malachi 3:6).

9. About the Jehovah's Witnesses

"The Jehovah's Witnesses forbid blood transfusions and quote a scripture in Acts to support their stance. I read that verse (Acts 15:29). It just mentioned 'blood.' Taking into context the entire Bible (especially the Old Testament), I would have thought that the 'blood' refers to animal blood, of which the OT Israelites were commanded not to partake. What specific resources or verses would you provide in this situation?"

Yes, the context certainly is the food laws of the Old Testament, which separated the Israelites from the theology and immorality of the Canaanites. (The health benefits were secondary to the real, theological issue.) Some people are eager to look for ways they can be distinct from others. I believe that this is what the Witnesses have done. By superficial study of a passage, which has led to their stand that blood transfusions are sinful (thus leading to a number of needless deaths), the Witnesses are able to be "one up" on other religious groups.

The resource I would point you to is your own Bible concordance. Do a study of the word "blood," especially in Leviticus and the other legal sections of the Old Testament. This is the background against which the dispute of Acts 15 makes sense. These were issues of the early Jewish Christians; they are not our issues.

10. Jehovah's Witnesses' Claims About the Kingdom

"Jehovah's Witnesses claim that the kingdom of God (invisible, apparently) is already here, and it is not the church. Are there different definitions of 'the kingdom,' and if so, which are relevant today?"

The Witnesses claim that Jesus came to earth to set up the kingdom, but failed. As a result, in the late nineteenth and early twentieth centuries, God secretly visited the earth and set up an invisible society, selecting his faithful witnesses, who now meet in "Kingdom Halls." Yes, there are different definitions or aspects to the kingdom, and disciples do not always speak clearly about the meanings.

- Kingdom = realm. In one sense, the realm of our King is the entire universe, and thus his kingdom is universal. Everyone is in it, whether or not they want to be!
- Kingdom = rule. In another sense, the kingdom comprises the willing subjects of the King. On earth this has special meaning for the church, since disciples make up the church.

For more on this, let me recommend a book to you: *The Reign of God,* written by Jim McGuiggan.[3]

11. Theodicy

"The following question comes from a relative whom I would like to help: 'Why would a God who is omnipresent, omnipotent and all-loving create people when he knows such a very small percent will choose to follow him, and the rest will be sent to hell?'"

Questions about why a just God tolerates evil are addressed by the branch of study known as "theodicy." Any problem with God's justice falls into this category. To begin with, it is not wrong to have these kinds of questions. In Genesis 18

Abraham struggled with God's justice in connection with Sodom and Gomorrah. Read the account carefully; the important point is not the percentage of the populace who "made it." The key issue is Abraham's faith in a just God as he exclaims, "Will not the Judge of all the earth do right?" (Genesis 18:25). And a number of other Biblical characters shared a similar concern. (See Jeremiah 12:1 and Habakkuk 1:3, for example.) To ask the question, even the most fundamental, bothersome question, is actually therapeutic, and to "stuff" the question may be injurious to your faith. In other words, part of maturing spiritually is being real enough to work through your concerns, even if, at the end of the day, they are only partly resolved.

Well, why *would* God create individuals (or allow them to be born) when he knows that they are not going to make it through to heaven at the end? The answer has something to do with free will and something to do with the meaning of goodness.

As human beings, we have the ability to make good choices, as well as to make bad ones. A moral universe is one where there is right and there is wrong. Moreover, it is possible for beings of free will to embrace good or to embrace evil. If it were not possible for me to do wrong, then why would I be praised as a good person? Goodness is possible for us humans when and only when we have a choice.

Sure, God could have chosen to create no one—no one with free will. No free will, no risk—but also, no people! Bottom line, creating people must have been worth it (and it must be better than the alternative of creating nothing). Otherwise God, who is always good, wouldn't have done as he did. Interestingly, you rarely hear critics who blame God for the world's injustice suggesting that he shouldn't have created them!

A final analogy is in order. Why do we choose to have children? Considering the possibility that they might embrace a life of crime or even turn against us, their fathers and mothers, why don't we just play it safe and decide not to procreate? It is worth it, for love.

12. Did God Create Evil?

"Since God created everything, did he create evil? I refuse to believe this, but I am left with no other thoughts. No matter what the answer, satisfying or not, I'll still not be so bold as to question the goodness of God. I'll simply have to wait until the day when all the hidden things of God are revealed."

You are right to insist on the goodness of God, just as Abram did in Genesis 18:25. The answer is that evil was not created, any more than good was created. Evil is what happens whenever free moral agents resist the will of God. And yet it does not exist, in and of itself. Our universe is not somehow dualistic, with two opposite forces—"good" and "evil"—keeping one another in some sort of cosmic balance. God is good. Whatever resists God's will is evil. Evil exists only where there is rebellion against God. God never *willed* that free moral agents choose evil. Are we going to blame God for the sinful choices we have made?

13. Reaching Jews

"What is the most effective way to share the gospel or study the Bible with someone who is Jewish (grew up going to synagogue in the United States)? Would it be best to start by looking at Old Testament prophecies about the Messiah, showing how Jesus fulfilled them, or should one simply start at the beginning of a *Guard the Gospel* or *First Principles* type of series and proceed from there?"

While I have some experience in helping Jews to become Christians, I am not sure I am the best person to answer this question. Yet I do not think beginning with a standard study series, or even beginning with messianic prophecies, is the best strategy in the US. Here are a few suggestions—hope they're helpful:

- Many Jews in the US do not believe in the Bible (Old Testament). Don't assume they do. In addition, many do not believe in God. It is essential to establish faith, and this takes time.

- Seeing a church of disciples—and their love (John 13:34)—is key. This will go a long way toward dispelling historical Jewish-Christian mistrust, so common in our society.
- Be a friend. Through the power of friendship and that of the gospel (1 Thessalonians 2:8), a number of Jews have become disciples in the kingdom of God.
- Make sure your own life is a light. Many Jews highly value family priorities, financial responsibility and a disciplined life.

14. Jesus and the Eastern Peoples

"My family is all Muslim. I, on the other hand, did not find any fulfillment in that religion. I now understand who Christ is. I have been challenged by many of my coworkers who are Muslim. I have also been put down for my belief in Christ. My question is: If Jesus had such a big impact on so many people while he was here on earth, where were the people of Eastern religions? Why weren't they impacted by Jesus? Is it fair to say that if the people of Eastern religions had seen and witnessed Jesus performing miracles, then they would have believed in him? And maybe then they would have passed that belief on to the generations of today?"

Your decision to follow Christ despite opposition is commendable. Your question shows that you are well aware that somewhere down the line, the early Christians failed to take the pure gospel everywhere in the world. Yet actually many of the Eastern peoples were affected by Jesus. The apostles preached all through the land where Islam later would take hold (six centuries later). Thomas even made it to India. Church history suggests that many of the Asians east of Israel remained faithful for many, many generations. They were not as caught up in church politics as were the Christians west of Israel.

Whether all the easterners would automatically have re-pented on seeing the miracles and hearing the Word, how-ever, is questionable. People must have the heart, the willing-ness, as well. Please take a look at Luke 16:19-31, the story of the rich man and Lazarus, and you will see exactly what I mean. It is indeed sad that the thread of true Christianity was lost somewhere along the way. The same challenge faces us today: to take the saving message into all nations.

15. 'Hebrew Israelites'

"Have you heard anything about the Hebrew Israelites and their doctrine? I am trying to gather any information on them. Much of their life and doctrine does not seem to match up, and women seem to take a secondary role in their belief structure."

Sorry, I am unfamiliar with the group. There are more than 22,000 "Christian" denominations and sects, and new groups are popping up every week. I would encourage you to do a Web search on the Internet for more information.

As far as I know, the true Israel—the first century rem-nant who embraced Christ through the ministry of the apostles (Romans 9:6, 1:16-17)—became part of the church. Theologically speaking, there are no Israelites today.

16. Continuity

"I live in a nation where the Orthodox Church has great power. They teach that the true church must have continu-ity, with consistent succession of members from person to person all the way back to the first century to the apostles. It's believed that the apostle Andrew himself wandered through this land and started the church (not clearly proved or disproved by historians), which now is the Ukrainian Orthodox (Russian Orthodox) church. It's said that only apostles and their physical successors link the apostolic church to the church of today. Please help me find scriptures that clarify that doctrine, not the church's institutional continuity, is important to God and for salvation."

Let me say at the outset that I agree with you. The continuity between our church and the first century church is doctrinal, not institutional. The thread that connects us to them is the Scriptures, not a supposed chain of physical successors of the apostles. The church is described as a building, not as a chain. In Ephesians 2 the foundation is apostolic. There are no apostles today. We can build on the foundation, of course, since through the apostolic Scriptures the foundation is firmly laid. But just as when we add a story to a home, we do not need to lay again the foundation; so when we plant a church, we do not lay the foundation all over again.

The early church devoted itself to the apostles' teaching (Acts 2:42). Yet even the apostles did not have the right to change the teaching. Galatians 2:11 is a powerful passage, as is Galatians 1:7-9. I would certainly make use of these passages to argue your point. One more helpful passage is Mark 3:31-35 which emphasizes that we are members of Jesus' spiritual family not by virtue of which group we are part of, but on the basis of our acceptance of God's will in our lives.

17. Capital Punishment Carried Out by Christians

"Romans 13 teaches us that the law is put into place by men under the authority of God. So if the death penalty is already in place for a particular offense, is it not the criminal who chooses his punishment when he commits the crime? I refer to Deuteronomy 21:20-22. Or is it that when man's law conflicts with God's law, it is considered null and void, and that we should not take away a man's chance at salvation regardless of the crime?"

According to the New Testament, we should not be surprised that the state may enforce capital punishment, based on Romans 13. If, as I suspect, you are asking about the permissibility of a Christian's carrying out the death penalty (viewing himself as an extension of the state and not as a private citizen taking the life of his fellow man), this is another matter. Opinions will differ. The main factors to consider are the teaching of the Scriptures *and* the conscience of the government agent who is asked to execute. So far, I know of no disciples in this unfortunate dilemma. Any time we go against our own consciences (Romans 14:23), we sin. And you are right; God's law supersedes man's law.

18. Putting God to the Test

"What does it mean to put God to the test when we pray for God to act? Isn't there a thin line here?"

Praying for God to act isn't necessarily putting God to the test. "Test," in this sense, is more like testing God's patience. There is a way children can ask their fathers for something without testing them, and somewhere there is another, more negative and faithless way, that crosses that thin line.

19. Sororities and Fraternities

"What is your advice for someone who wants to become part of a sorority or fraternity?"

I think it depends on the nature of the sorority or fraternity. Loyalty to Christ must never come second. Neither family, fraternity, nor government has the right to ask for unconditional allegiance and obedience. (Interestingly, many have become disciples out of ministries within fraternities.) In my view, the more groups or associations that true Christians can influence, the better. Here are a few suggestions:

- Decide whether you can be a member of the group without compromising your conscience.
- Decide whether you can realistically afford any dues or other financial obligations that may be involved.
- If you are going to join, be determined that you will share your faith within the fraternity or sorority.

- Determine whether involvement in the group *and* in the local congregation may compromise your academic standing.

Paul's statement in 1 Corinthians 7:20 may be helpful. "Each one should remain in the situation which he was in when God called him." Using the principle we find here, there are those who believe there is a big difference in a person who becomes a disciple after being in a fraternity and one who would join a fraternity as a disciple. If you already have an established place in the group and then become a disciple, it may be a very different experience from coming in and going through the initiation as a believer.

In any case, get lots of advice from those who know you well. Talk with other brothers and sisters who have been members of fraternities and sororities. Their perspectives will be more valuable than mine.

20. Pain and Suffering

"Recently, I've had discussions with two women stuck on one question: 'If God is so good and loving, why is there so much pain and suffering for innocent people?' Each time I came away feeling like somehow I'd been defeated in the conversations. In the end, I came to the realization that there must be some level of faith involved in order to believe that God is good and does care. How should I respond to this question? What scriptures should I be going to?"

Questions about God's justice strike at the very heart of us all. You don't need to feel defeated; the Bible is immensely helpful with questions about evil and suffering. Yet the Scriptures never give pat answers—this is our temptation as we strive to bring clarity or solace to those affected by suffering. Since I addressed the question of theodicy earlier in question 11 in this section of the book, let me here provide you with a list of passages that have helped me to deal with the problem personally before summarizing my perspective:

- Genesis 3:16-17—Suffering is increased because we are in a fallen world into which sin has made a dramatic, and often catastrophic, entrance.
- Job 1-42—Spiritual growth can take place through suffering even if we *never* receive the explanation for why it has come into our lives. (Job never did find out why he suffered so.) Also: Beware of shallow and fallacious explanations about suffering. The erroneous theology of Eliphaz, Bildad and Zophar was roundly rebuked by the Lord.
- John 9:1-3—Suffering provides an opportunity for God to be glorified.
- Romans 5:3-4—When we persevere through suffering, character is built.
- Romans 8:18—Our present sufferings are not worth comparing with the glory that will be revealed in us.
- Revelation 21-22—One day there will be an end to suffering.

Christianity offers no comprehensive *explanation* to suffering, much less a promise of *exemption* from suffering—otherwise people would be coming into the church in droves! Yet it does promise grace to endure suffering and assures us that, through the cross, God himself has fully shown his heart and his competence to address the problem of evil in the most intimate way possible.

21. Bible Versions

"Every time I've heard you speak, you have recommended reading other versions of the Bible than the New International Version (NIV). Could you provide a list of the most popular and best translations? Could you also describe why some translations are better than others?"

The real question when it comes to most translations is, better for what—better for readability, better for serious study, or better for the majority of the group? I have read the Bible through nearly thirty times now, and I love to vary the version from reading to reading. I encourage you to experiment![4]

22. The New Testament and Aristotle

"Is it true that the earliest copies of the New Testament are from around 125 AD, only about twenty-five years later than the date the originals were written? Is it also true that the earliest copies of Aristotle's works are from around 1100 AD, or about 1400 years later than the time Aristotle lived?"

The oldest surviving NT manuscript does date to around 110-125 AD. (I have seen the papyrus fragment with my eyes and touched it with my hands!) As the New Testament was completed somewhere between 70 and 95 AD (give or take), the gap is only about one or two generations. In Aristotle's case, from 340 BC to 1100 AD (date of manuscripts), the gap is more than 1400 years. This is not a span of one or two generations, but more than fifty generations! The textual evidence is one reason we can trust in the accuracy of the Scriptures.[5]

23. Paul's Tone

"In his letters, Paul was always inspiring and warm yet serious. In Romans 6:7-23, Paul was rather 'different.' What's the significance of this passage?"

I assume you're asking about the significance of Romans 6 in relation to Paul's tone or demeanor, not its theological meaning. I think it is interesting that you are sensitive to the *feel* a passage or letter may have, because most readers act as though there are no distinctions at all. Yet the Spirit has spoken through human individuals speaking human languages against cultural backgrounds and out of their own personal experiences. This fact in no way invalidates the inspiration of the Bible, yet it is important to note if we are to get the most out of our Bible study.

Yes, I think Paul is usually warm and serious—as all of us should aim to be. Yet he is not always this way. There are times that he dispenses with the warmth (the introductory section of Galatians) and other times that his tone moves from heavy to light (all of which serves the more serious purposes behind his writing). As for Romans 6, I personally do not think Paul is less warm or serious here than in the rest of Romans. Possibly because he is dealing with the Biblical mandate to radical change—living by the Spirit instead of by the flesh—we find this challenging.

24. Unbelieving Jews

"What are your thoughts on the letter to the Romans and the fate of the Jews who do not believe in Jesus? Will they be saved just by being God's people, even though they don't believe in Jesus?"

Not at all! As Paul argues in Romans 9-11, only those Jews who follow the Messiah are the people of God (9:6). The Jews who rejected Jesus in the first century were *not* the people of God. They were not part of the remnant of faithful Jews, which included, among others, Mary (the mother of Jesus), Elizabeth, Zechariah, Anna and Simeon. After the first century, no Jew was reckoned among God's people.

In Romans Paul is answering the question about the situation of the Jews in *his* day, not ours! Evangelicals err when they squeeze some twenty-first century fulfillment out of Romans 9-11, prophesying a mass conversion of the nation of Israel. What comfort would it have been to Paul's reader if he said, in effect, "Don't worry about all your (Jewish) friends and relatives; two thousand years from now all living Jews will make it"? Paul himself is an example of a Jew who would be saved in the remnant (Romans 10-11). "All Israel" means all *true* Jews—those who accept Christ—and no others. Today the door is closed. We do not expect a mass conversion of the Jews, nor did Paul ever predict one.

25. Birth Control

"Is birth control unrighteous? I read in Genesis 38:8-10 where Onan 'spilled his semen on the ground to keep from producing offspring for his brother. What he did was wicked in the Lord's sight.'"

The sin of Onan was his refusal to fulfill his duty to his brother to provide an heir. (See Deuteronomy 25:5-10.) The passage really has nothing at all to do with birth control, even though the Catholic church has traditionally used it as a proof text against birth control.

The subject of birth control is, for the most part, a matter of opinion. As long as no conception has taken place, the ethical issues are simple. When an egg *has* been fertilized (the opposite of the Onan situation), the embryo is an incipient human being. But then your question did not concern abortion, RU-486, etc.

26. Family Planning

"To me, natural family planning is a form of contraception. I have looked in several Catholic theology defense books, including the recent catechism, but could not locate any Biblical defense for natural family planning instead of contraception. Please provide any background for the development of this doctrine."

The influence of Gnosticism on the second century church drove it ultimately to overreact to sexuality. Many Gnostics saw the body as basically evil, and therefore pleasure derived from the body was seen as unspiritual. In other words, sex was to be "procreational," and never "recreational," even within the marriage union. This, of course, contradicts the overwhelming tone of Song of Songs and the clear teaching of passages like Proverbs 5:19.

The Bible itself is absolutely silent on the matter of any method of birth control. Though the evolution of the Roman Catholic position on birth control is well documented (I would encourage you to study the patristic writers), we do not accept the authority of the church as an institution, which is changing and fallible, but rather, only the authority of God's word.

27. 'Q'

"I recently read of books called 'Q' and the gospel of Thomas. Interesting reading! What do you think of them and their authenticity? Why are they not included in the Bible?"

Actually, much of "Q"—the hypothetical source of material common to Matthew and Luke—*is* in the New Testament. Let me recommend that you read an introduction to the New Testament (e.g. Merrill Tenney's *New Testament Survey*). You will then be able to answer the first part of your question.

As for the gospel of Thomas, it is a Gnostic work dating from after the time of the New Testament. This is one reason it is not "included." And, as you will have realized from reading it, there are a number of contradictions with the New Testament. (For example, the Gospel of Thomas teaches that women are not worthy of eternal life and that esoteric knowledge is how we become spiritual.) This spurious document has no connection with the true apostle Thomas, who faithfully followed the teachings of his Master, most likely establishing the church in India and dying there for the faith.

28. Gods (Little 'g')

"In John 10 Jesus confronts the Jews who are upset about his claiming to be God's Son. He quotes a psalm that calls people 'gods' because the word of God came to them. A friend of mine believes that Jesus is saying that everybody is a god, 'so don't be upset about me. I'm just like you. We're all gods.' What's a good answer for this?"

Good question—and no need to be taken in by your friend's fallacious reasoning! The "gods" of Psalm 82 are simply human beings in positions of leadership. I know this explanation at first will sound strange, so please bear with me. The passage reads,

> God presides in the great assembly;
>   he gives judgment among the "gods":
> "How long will you defend the unjust

and show partiality to the wicked?
Defend the cause of the weak and fatherless;
    maintain the rights of the poor and oppressed.
Rescue the weak and needy;
    deliver them from the hand of the wicked.
"They know nothing, they understand nothing.
    They walk about in darkness;
    all the foundations of the earth are shaken.
"I said, 'You are "gods";
    you are all sons of the Most High.'
But you will die like mere men;
    you will fall like every other ruler."
Rise up, O God, judge the earth,
    for all the nations are your inheritance.
(Psalm 82:1-8)

It is extremely important to study the context of a passage before ever coming to a conclusion about what it means or what its terms (like "gods") may mean. Here the Lord is expressing his indignation against wicked rulers. They do not champion the cause of the poor. Now insofar as these men are sons of God, they are "gods." In the Bible, "gods" normally means "false gods," the objects of idolatry (Genesis 31:19). But in this passage, it specifies "political rulers." Despite their arrogance, they will die "like every other ruler." The word "other" implies that they themselves are rulers.

As Jesus said in John 10:34-35, "...'Is it not written in your Law, "I have said you are gods"? If he called them "gods," to whom the word of God came—and the Scripture cannot be broken...,'" these are those to whom the word of God came, in other words, human beings.

Sorry, human beings are *not* God. This has been mankind's struggle—the will to personal autonomy, as though he were the center of the universe—since Eden (Genesis 3).

Anyway, that is the answer. I am not so sure, however, that your friend (who sounds influenced by New Age thinking) will appreciate it, since it is somewhat "advanced." It would be better to get him or her reading the gospel of John—really reading it, not just grabbing at support for erroneous theology.

29. Annulment

"There has been a lot of talk recently about the show, 'Who Wants to Marry a Millionaire?' and the likely pending annulment case. Is there any Biblical basis for an annulment? I know of none. How and when did this doctrine develop in the Catholic church?"

I know of none, either. Sorry, I do not know the origin of "annulment," except as a concession to the law of the Bible that divorce, in most cases, is wrong. This is the sort of doctrine that would have made Jesus' blood boil. (I am thinking particularly of his assault on Corban theology in Mark and his attack on oaths in Matthew 23.) As usual, we humans try to create loopholes. I think it is like the Calvinist proclaiming, "Since that fellow left the Lord, he was never saved in the first place."

30. Metaphysics

"What is your understanding of metaphysics, and how would you study the Bible with someone who believes in it?"

Metaphysics, traditionally understood, is the study of truth *beyond* (meta) physics. Metaphysics is a synonym of philosophy. In my experience, many people who talk about metaphysics are simply trying to impress others, and I would encourage us all to take a look at Colossians 2:4 and 2:8. Human reasoning alone is bound to fail, nor can it save our souls. It is like trying to pull yourself up by your own bootstraps, and it is exceedingly popular these days.

Notes

[1] If you want a quicker read, see chapter 8 of my *True & Reasonable, New and Expanded Edition*.

[2] If you want to see how the current pope handles this, read his book, *Crossing the Threshold of Hope* (New York: Knopf, 1994), 6. John Paul II is aware of the contradiction with Jesus' command to call no one "father," yet his solution is to affirm that we must not be afraid of this practice (even though Jesus said not to do it) because it is deeply rooted in Roman Catholic tradition.

[3] Jim McGuiggan, *The Reign of God* (Fort Worth: Star Bible Publications, 1992), phone: 1-800-433-7507.

[4] Please see the chart on page 173 in my book *The God Who Dared* for more information. Also see the chapter on translations in Steve Kinnard's book *Getting the Most from the Bible* (Woburn, Mass.: DPI, 2000).

[5] For more on this, please see my book *True and Reasonable* or visit the archived material in *The Bible on Trial* at Aces Online.

5

Essays

1
The Trinity

No Simple Doctrine

This paper attempts to explain the doctrine of the trinity. Maybe it's my high church past or my instinctive distrust of the abstractions of medieval theology, but something about the doctrine of the trinity just feels contrived—it's just too neat, too simple. (Or maybe it's too deep for my shallow mind!) Yet I know I must not shirk my authorial duty; moreover, it's good to push oneself. I like what C. S. Lewis said:

> If Christianity was something we were making up, of course we would make it easier. But it is not. We cannot compete, in simplicity, with people who are inventing religions. How could we? We are dealing with Fact. Of course anyone can be simple if he has no facts to bother about.[1]

We are indeed concerned with the facts, with sifting truth and error. The truth is, the trinity is not the sort of doctrine inventors of religions would concoct—which is one reason it may have the ring of truth to it. And though I rarely use the term "trinity," in my opinion, as I shall attempt to show, the doctrine does give as good an explanation of the nature of the godhead as anything man has come up with.

What Is the Trinity?

The OED (Oxford English Dictionary) defines "trinity": "Being three; group of three. From Latin *trinitas,* 'triad.'" Surely, the persons of the trinity are not distinct persons like the Three Musketeers, the Three Stooges, the Three Tenors or the Three Little Pigs. On the other hand, we aren't simply dealing with one person in three roles, like a person who functions as mother, wife and professional. The first error to be avoided is tritheism, three separate gods; the second is modalism, where God "morphs" from one form to another according to the need of the hour.

Part of coming to terms with the doctrine is grasping what theologians mean when they discuss the "persons" of the trinity. In modern English "three persons" strongly implies a triad of gods. But the theological term "person" is from the Latin *persona,* which means "mask, part or character," as in the characters of a play. This of course does not mean that God is somehow "pretending," like an actor.[2]

In brief, the Holy Trinity is the three-in-one.

Biblical Basis

Often the Father, Son and Spirit are mentioned together in the New Testament (2 Corinthians 13:14, Matthew 28:19, John 14:17-23).[3] They are three in personality but one in nature or essence. Father, Son and Spirit are each God (in essence), but none can be identified with the other.

Again, we must guard ourselves against false understandings of trinity, or else we will drift into either the errors of "unitarianism" (which roundly rejects the trinity) or the errors of tritheism. (The Qur'an mistakes belief in the trinity for tritheism when it condemns "Those who say Allah is three."[4])

In short, all three persons are divine. Obviously, our heavenly Father is God.[5] In addition, many verses state that Christ is divine (2 Peter 1:1, Titus 2:13, John 1:1, 14), not to mention the indirect proofs of his deity, such as his forgiveness of man's sins (Mark 2) and claiming as his own the name of God (John 8:58). But how can Christ have two natures simultaneously? An illustration may help. Orange juice is 100% wet, and yet it is also 100% citrus. It isn't somehow half wet and half citrus—it's wholly both at the same time. In the same way, Jesus is human *and* God.[6]

Finally, it is also clear from the Scriptures that the Spirit, the third person of the trinity, or the "Spirit of God," is divine. Let's check out the OED definition of the Spirit: "The active essence or essential power of the Deity, conceived as a creative, animating or inspiring influence." Now this may be an accurate definition, but how does it help us be closer to God? It makes a difference in our lives only when we sense and appreciate that God, through his[7] Spirit, is living within us (John 14). The Spirit in nature is God;[8] all members of the trinity are equally divine.

Trinity in Church History

The earlier "ecumenical councils" strove to define and describe the relationships between the members of the godhead (Nicea in 325, Constantinople in 381 and Chalcedon in 451, to mention a few). Yes, many believers in the early Christian era spent generations hammering out the doctrine of the trinity, investigating the intricacies of the Spirit. Even in the Middle Ages, interest in the trinity was strong. Aquinas produced the most thorough treatise on "The Blessed Trinity."[9]

In the Restoration movement, especially in the nineteenth century, there was a reaction against trinitarian language. The famous hymn "Holy, Holy, Holy" mentions "God in three persons, blessèd Trinity!"[10] And yet in the overreaction to "traditional" doctrines, these words were changed to "God over all and blessed eternally." Was this really necessary? Is it not true that Father, Son and Spirit are all divine?

Analogies Good and Bad

While it is true that Father, Son and Spirit are all God, we cannot correctly say that the Father is the Son, or that Spirit and Son are interchangeable. Analogies therefore need to be carefully selected, lest we inadvertently support false doctrine through our attempts to refute it.

The analogy I most often use to explain the trinity is the analogy of the amorphous forms of H_2O. Ice = water; liquid water = water; and steam = water (in essence); but ice ≠ steam; ice ≠ liquid water; and liquid water ≠ steam. Though I like the water analogy, its shortcoming is that it implies the false doctrine of modalism, that God appears in one form now, another at another time.[11] I have heard worse analogies: time (past, present and future), even an egg (shell, white and yolk).

Opponents of trinity ask, how can 1 + 1 + 1 = 1? But the mathematics is all wrong. Really it's a case of 1^3: 1 x 1 x 1 = 1. Moving from simple math to geometry, the triangular illustration may better encapsulate the truth about the relations among the persons of the trinity.

Triangular Illustration[12]

As someone put it more academically, "A better illustration based in human nature would be, as suggested earlier, the relation between our mind, its ideas and the expression of these ideas in words. There is obviously a unity among all three of these without there being an identity. In this sense, they illustrate the trinity."[13]

No single analogy captures the divine mystery, though the various pictures will be more convincing to different people.

Trinity and Our Walk with God

The doctrine of the trinity has been firmly established. Let me now suggest some ways in which understanding trinity illuminates our walk with the Lord:

1. Trinity brings us great assurance. The Father is God above us, the Son is God beside us, and the Spirit is God within us.
2. Trinity helps us to see that God is love. How could God have been (eternally) love if he had no one to love? But as Augustine commented, love always existed among the members of the trinity. This theme has often been elevated and discussed in our century by C. S. Lewis and Francis Schaeffer. The three-in-one God is a divine family, in which perfect love has always been exchanged.
3. Respect for the trinity deepens our humility, as we see God's transcendence. As Isaiah says (Isaiah 55:8-9), his ways are not our ways, and there is an unfathomable distance between his ways and wisdom and our own. (See also Romans 11:33-36.)

Summary

If the whole concept seems complicated, don't fret! If theologians struggled for centuries to put the divine mystery into words, and if you cannot manage it in half an hour, I wouldn't be too concerned! To wrap it all up, all this does *not* mean that:

- There are three gods (tritheism).
- We are normally to pray to Jesus or pray to the Spirit. In John 16:23-26 Jesus explains that we are to pray to the Father in his name, although occasionally in the New Testament prayer is also addressed to the Lord Jesus (e.g. Acts 7:59).
- God "morphs" from one person to another (modalism). The persons of the trinity always remain distinct.
- This little chapter is the last word on the subject! God cannot be put in a box.

It *does,* however, mean that:

- Trinity is Biblical. Whether or not the word itself appears in the New Testament, it is valid. (Even the word "Bible" does not occur in the Bible, yet it is a completely functional and useful term.)
- God's nature is a mystery—and so we will always have to strive to our utmost to embrace and accept the nature of God in our lives.
- We need to dig deeper into the word of God if we are going to go higher in our walk with him.

Holy, Holy, Holy!

Despite my initial apprehension, my study has led me to accept the time-honored doctrine of the Holy Trinity. Returning to the corrections made to the old hymn, I do not mean to dispute the words "God over all and blessed eternally," for he is. Yet it is wholly unnecessary to distance ourselves from the original wording of the song. Its final verse spoke the truth perfectly well:

> Holy, holy, holy! Lord God Almighty!
> All thy works shall praise thy name,
> in earth, and sky, and sea;
> Holy, holy, holy! Merciful and mighty!
> God in three persons, blessèd Trinity!

Notes

[1] C. S. Lewis, *Mere Christianity* (New York: The Macmillan Company, 1943), 145.

[2] Theatergoers, think about the term *Dramatis personae.*

[3] Several religions have "trinities." Hinduism has Shiva, Vishnu and Brahma. The Druids had Taranis, Esus and Teutates. The ancient Egyptians also had their trinity. Yet, unlike the Biblical trinity, these "trinities" are triads of gods, not one triune god.

[4] Islamic accusations denied that God, Jesus and Mary were gods. This clearly reflects the exalted, and erroneous, position of Mary in the seventh century AD.

[5] For further reading on the nature and divinity of God, see Edwin A. Abbot, *Flatland* (Oxford: Blackwell, 1875); J. I. Packer, *Knowing God* (Downers Grove: InterVarsity, 1975); Francis A. Schaeffer, *He Is There and He Is Not Silent* (Wheaton, Ill.: Tyndale House, 1972); and *The God Who Is There* (Downers Grove: InterVarsity Press, 1968).

[6] For further reading on the nature and divinity of the Son of God, see William Barclay, *The Mind of Jesus* (New York: Harper & Row, 1961); Charles Edward Jefferson, *Jesus—the Same* (Woburn, Mass.: DPI, 1997; original edition 1908); *Jesus with the People*, ed. Jones & Jones (Woburn, Mass.: DPI, 1996); and Philip Yancey, *The Jesus I Never Knew* (Grand Rapids: Zondervan, 1995).

[7] We will not join the feminist dialogue about the gender of God, whom the Bible consistently describes as a "he." Interestingly, I have never heard a feminist lobby for a pronoun change for Satan—the devil is always "he"!

[8] For further reading on the nature and divinity of the Spirit, see Frederick Dale Bruner, *A Theology of the Holy Spirit* (London: Hodder & Stoughton, 1970); Douglas Jacoby, *The Spirit*; and John R. W. Stott, *Baptism and Fullness* (London: InterVarsity Press, 1975).

[9] See Thomas Aquinas (1225-1274), *Summa Theologica.*

[10] Bishop R. Heber, 1783-1826.

[11] Worse, that the Father is "harder" than the Son, the Spirit more ethereal than both, and so forth!

[12] In my understanding of trinity, the trinitarian triangle may not be totally equilateral!

[13] Norman L. Geisler and Abdul Saleeb, *Answering Islam* (Grand Rapids: Baker, 1993), 269.

2
What Does the Bible Really Say About Women?

by Douglas Jacoby
with the assistance of Patricia Gempel
(1990, revised 1999)

Does the Bible really teach that women are inferior to men? Was the apostle Paul a blatant woman-hater? And after all, wasn't the Bible a product of a male chauvinist society? Unfortunately there is great confusion in the minds of men and women concerning the woman's role in Christianity. Misapplication of Scripture, coupled with the secular campaign for female liberation, has intensified the confusion, leading many women into fear, discontent or rebellion.

We need to learn God's will about the woman's role so that we can be free from the confusion and thus free to follow God's plan for our lives. Matthew 11:28-30 tells us that God's plan is not burdensome, but rather, a flight of freedom for our souls. Still, we often find it difficult to trust God's word and practice it in our lives.

Our article aims to correct common misunderstandings about women and the Bible, and to present the truth about the woman's role. As we will see, there is no reason whatever to reject the authority of the Bible because of its teaching on women. Actually, this is one of the strongest arguments for accepting its inspiration!

The Honor of Women in the Bible

Contrary to the claims of some, women in the Bible have generally been highly honored. Let's discuss the theme of the dignity and honor of women in the Bible, beginning with God, moving on to Jesus, then considering the general commendation women receive in the Scriptures.

God the Father

The source of the high honor given to women is found in God himself. God makes no distinction between man and woman as far as their basic dignity goes. He created both. Both have rebelled equally against his will, and he lovingly receives both back to himself on the same conditions of faith and repentance. Jesus died on the cross for *all* people, and Christians have been given a commission to share the good news with both men and women (Mark 16:15). Moreover, God expects total commitment from all alike. Truly, God shows no favoritism (Acts 10:34).

Scripture makes it perfectly clear that the creation of woman was not an afterthought. Woman is just as much a special part of God's creation as man. However, it is tragic that the prevailing attitude in the world toward women has been negative and even demeaning. A popular Chinese proverb calls baby girls "maggots in the rice bowl," and the government cruelly translates this belief into policy in this nation of 1.2 billion. The Apocrypha (officially accepted as an inspired addition to the Bible by nearly a billion people today) states, "...the birth of a daughter is a loss."[1] Hundreds of millions of women on earth are routinely abused, shouted at, sworn at, bullied and beaten every day. What a contrast the Bible presents, from the very first page.

People will ask, "Is God male or female?" Interestingly, in one sense the answer to the question is yes! Genesis 1:27 says

> So God created man in his own image,
>   in the image of God he created him;
>   male and female he created them.

The "image" of God is reflected in both male and female! We are taught to address God as "Father," and certainly this is appropriate, but did you know that our heavenly Father's personality has all of the best attributes of male and female? God has the perfect blend of love, power, sensitivity, strength, emotion, rationality, concern, decisiveness, patience and thoughtfulness. This is why men and women are complementary. God never intended for them to stand *independent* of each other. On the contrary, he created them to be *interdependent* (1 Corinthians 11:11).

Jesus Christ

No one has done more to liberate women than Jesus Christ. In an age when many females were ranked as equal to slaves, Jesus acknowledged their worth and elevated their status to equality with males before God. The Gospels record numerous accounts of Christ interacting with women on the same level as he did with men.

Jesus had close relationships with women (John 11:5), supported them when others put them down (Luke 7:36-50, Mark 14:3-9) and taught them personally (Luke 10:39). Jesus' ministry was financed by women (Luke 8:3). His first post-resurrection appearance was to women (Matthew 28:1-10). Jesus Christ did not hesitate to break through racial, traditional and sexual barriers—to the utter amazement of his followers (John 4:9, 27). Though not compromising on the need for women to repent, Jesus upheld the honor and dignity of womanhood. Let it never be said that the Christian religion robs women of their dignity!

Of Heroes and Heroines

The Bible is full of heroes—great men of faith—but it is also full of heroines. The Old Testament has Sarah, Rebecca, Rachel, Deborah, Ruth, Hannah, Esther and a host of others. In the New Testament, we quickly recall Mary (the mother of Jesus) and Mary Magdalene. But there are so many more heroines—for example, the Samaritan woman (John 4), Priscilla (Acts 18), Lydia (Acts 16) and the woman who anointed Jesus with perfume (Mark 14). The Bible writers weren't afraid to give women the credit they deserved.

Men Have Much to Learn

Some people have interpreted the Bible to mean that men have nothing to learn from women. It is true that the New Testament does not allow women to usurp (or wrongfully take) authority from men in teaching or preaching (1 Timothy 2), but nothing could be further from the truth than to say that men have nothing to learn from women.

For example, in Genesis 21:12, God told Abraham to, "Listen to whatever Sarah tells you…." Sarah was his wife and was commended for her submissive attitude toward him (1 Peter 3), but in that instance God told Abraham to listen to his wife. Deborah was a judge over Israel, and through her wisdom many difficult issues were decided (Judges 4:5). Priscilla was a trusted companion in the apostle Paul's ministry (Acts 18) and several times received his commendation. These examples could be multiplied many times over. The point is clear: Men are not considered intellectually, morally or spiritually better than women in the Bible.

Christian Chauvinism?

Is it true that women are degraded or downgraded in the Bible? Middle Eastern society today is much the same as Jesus' society was two thousand years ago. Most Middle Eastern nations today are Muslim, so for the sake of illustration, let's consider the position of the Koran on women:

> Men have authority over women because Allah has made the one superior to the other, and because they spend their wealth to maintain them. Good women are obedient. (Surah 4)

Mohammed goes on to reprimand disobedient wives: they are to be rebuked, beaten and sent to bed! In most mosques the women are hidden behind a screen. Heaven in Islam is "a band of brothers," and little thought is given to women. This is degrading, but thankfully, this is not the teaching of the Bible. Pakistan severely restricts the rights of women, not allowing them on the streets at night. This is a radical Islamic republic. In another Muslim nation, Saudi Arabia, women are not allowed to drive cars. If these comments are hard to relate to, rent a copy of *Not Without My Daughter* and prepare to see how women are treated in many countries of the world (in this case, the fundamentalist Islamic republic of Iran). Women's rights are virtually nonexistent. And the sad stories can easily be multiplied worldwide.[2]

If the Bible were really only the product of men, we would expect it to treat women in the manner of first century society. Instead, we find a nice surprise: women in Jesus' day would have enjoyed *more,* not *less,* honor if their husbands and society followed the principles of God's word. The same holds true today.

Submission

Our society instinctively distrusts authority and submission. That's why so many people dislike the Bible's teaching on marriage. Marriage is designed to operate on the principle of loving "submission" (the wife's side) and loving "leadership" (the husband's side). This is God's plan. No wonder the state of marriage in the world is such a disaster! People have tried every way but God's way.

The Dirty Word

"Submission" has become the dirty word in our society. Men and women simply do not *want* to submit, and signs of rebellion are everywhere. Students disrespect teachers, citizens hold police and other authorities in contempt, and children disobey parents. It shouldn't surprise us that our society, with its selfish emphasis on "me," has rejected God's plan for submission within marriage. God never said it is easy to give up our rights and put the needs of others ahead of our own, but he commanded us to do that because he knows that it is only through self-denial that we will find self-fulfillment (Philippians 2:4-7). He has created us "to do good works" and to function on the fuel of sacrificial love (Ephesians 2:10, 5:1-2). Selfish ambition is on the Galatians 5 list of sins because it destroys love and relationships.

Submission does not mean domination or oppression. The Bible teaches very clearly against abuse of authority (Matthew 20:25, Colossians 3:18-19). There are two correct meanings of submission, and neither of them usually settles very well when we hear it for the first time. The first is to *willingly* put the needs of another (male or female) ahead of our own, as in Ephesians 5:21: "Submit to one another out of reverence for Christ." The second meaning is to willingly subject ourselves to another's authority, as in the Hebrews 13:17 command of submission to the authority of church leaders. This also applies to the relationship of wives to husbands.

This last area tends to be the most difficult to digest. Today's society interprets the submission of a woman to a man as an admission of inferiority. To make things worse, some men have abused their positions in leadership and have become tyrants. Still others lack confidence in gaining female respect. The result can be rebellion at the seeming unfairness of the woman's role.

Viewing the situation from God's perspective, however, puts submission in a positive light. The Lord, not man, has designed marriage, knowing what will make it work best. He put submission into the relationship to create order, not inferiority. Someone has to be the leader, and God gave that responsibility to the husband. A man's authority over his wife is not earned; it is assigned by God. Submitting to that authority does not mean he is superior and she is inferior, it simply fulfills responsibility within the different roles God has assigned both.

One more thing: while most women do not like having to "submit" to a man, it is also true that many women find it even *more* difficult to submit to a woman. The real issue is submission, not gender. (Of course, at the bottom of it all lies rebellion against the authority of God himself.)

Equality = Equalization?

Does equality mean that men and women should be the same in every respect? Consider a soccer team: since everyone is "equal," should we erase the distinction between the positions and let *everyone* play goalkeeper? Or let everyone play any position he likes? This would not increase the chance of winning in the slightest! Teamwork is essential, and this is possible only when all the players operate within the roles assigned to them. "Equalization" would destroy any hope of victory.

There are several basic differences between men and women (physical size and strength, voice, childbearing, emotional makeup), but the differences between the sexes go even further: we have different roles as well. We certainly need to accept the basic differences, but we also need to understand the difference in roles. God's plan, especially in the marriage relationship, is for men and women to complement one another. We must remember that men and women were never intended to stand independent of each other. God's word clearly teaches that the husband is to be the spiritual leader of the family (Genesis 3:16). The Bible says, "Wives, submit to your husbands as to the Lord" (Ephesians 5:22).

On the other hand, the husband is not free to be uncaring, lazy or disrespectful (Ephesians 5:25-33). In fact, he is commanded to love his wife "just as Christ loved the church and gave himself up for her" (Ephesians 5:25). We seriously wonder if a wife would object to following her husband's lead if his attitude was one of sensitive, sacrificial, selfless devotion to her.

Differences in roles absolutely do *not* imply inferiority or superiority. Of course, we are all equal in one sense in our standing before God, but *equality* before God does not mean *equalization* of our different God-assigned roles. We can fill different roles and functions and still remain "equal." All church members share one sort of equality (the ground is level at the foot of the cross), but it would be incorrect to say everyone is equally a leader. In the same way, the Bible teaches that men and women are equal (Galatians 3:28), but that does not override the role differences between husband and wife.

Summary

Submission does not mean inferiority. Rather, it is the means to harmonious relationships. Our society is totally fixated on individual rights and has overreacted to the Biblical concept of submission. The right balance is what will bring the harmony and depth of friendship we all seek.

The 'Woman Hater'

The mistaken notion that Paul was a woman-hater is based on a very few passages from his letters and a whole lot of bad will on the part of people with an ax to grind. Before we examine the passages taken to show Paul's "male chauvinism," let's examine his general attitude toward women from the evidence.

If Paul were negative toward women, his own writings should be highly incriminating. Yet when we study those writings, we find a character exactly opposite to that which we have been led to expect! He made his appreciation and praise of women clear in every letter he wrote:

- *Rome:* Paul's warm feelings toward women friends and colleagues exude from the printed page (Romans 16).
- *Corinth:* He allows women to pray and prophesy in the assembly (1 Corinthians 11) and says all apostles have a right to marry (1 Corinthians 9:5). The demand for a celibate clergy is vigorously rejected! (See 1 Timothy 4:3.)
- *Galatia:* Paul strongly upholds the equality of all believers: "There is neither...male nor female, for you are all one in Christ Jesus" (Galatians 3:28).
- *Philippi:* Paul urges the men to support the female leadership in the church (Philippians 4:3).
- *Colosse:* Paul teaches husbands to sacrificially love their wives (Ephesians 5). To the Colossians he says, "Husbands, love your wives and do not be harsh with them" (Colossians 3:19).

- *Thessalonica:* Paul encourages the Christians to respect everyone who works hard in the church—not just the men (1 Thessalonians 5:12).
- *Ephesus and Crete:* When Paul writes to male leaders, he is fully supportive of the women's role. Men are to expect a high standard of commitment from the women, just as from the men (Titus 2:3-5), and yet they need to treat them with sensitivity and respect (1 Timothy 5:2). In fact, Paul reserves the highest leadership positions in the local church for *married* men with well-behaved children (1 Timothy 3, Titus 1). Clearly he appreciated the invaluable experience and insight that come only from a smoothly running Christian marriage in which both partners communicate, love each other (love God even more) and fill the roles God has assigned them.

It is obvious that, far from being insensitive to women, Paul was extremely considerate. In fact, when we tally all of Paul's personal greetings in his letters, *a full forty percent are to women*—that's better than most men do today. Some woman-hater!

Of course, it is possible to say one thing in a letter and yet be different in person. Exactly what was Paul's personal effect on the women of his day? Consider the upper-class Greek women in his society—the ones most likely to be offended if he was "down on women." As we read Acts, which records the growth of the early church, we see many noblewomen coming to faith and following Paul (Acts 16:13-14, 17:4, 17:12, 17:34, etc.). They weren't offended by the "woman-hater"—instead, they accepted him and his message.

Problematic Passages?

Now that we have an accurate view of Paul's attitude toward women, we can examine the passages problematic for those who have been offended by him. People have taken 1 Corinthians 14:34 to mean that women must keep absolutely silent in the church. The situation was that some women were embarrassing their husbands and violating order and decorum by arguing with men over the interpretation of prophecies. (This is the context of 1 Corinthians 14.) Paul tells them to take up their questions *outside* the assembly, once they have gone home. The difficulty with the view that Paul prohibits women to speak at all is that in chapter 11, he evidently has no objection to women praying and talking out loud in the services.

1 Timothy 2:11 teaches the same principle. Verse 12, however, deserves comment: "I do not permit a woman to teach or to have authority over a man; she must be silent." As we have seen, Paul is not commanding total silence. Nor does he say this because men are superior to women. He does, however, uphold the Biblical principle that in the church, the men are to lead. What a shame that in most churches today there are few men who attend, and even fewer who take on leadership responsibility. Far from liking to dominate in the church, most men have little or no desire to be spiritual leaders. In such a setting, it is easy for a woman to want to take over the leadership. God commands that she not do so.

Paul's Insight and God's

It is God's word that pierces our inner being and lays bare our thoughts and attitudes (Hebrews 4). Paul's writings (thirteen of the twenty-seven New Testament books) are *all* inspired. Paul had a profound understanding of human character, including female character. He was right when he commented on the weak will and lack of self-control on the part of many women (2 Timothy 3:6-7). Women on the average *are* much more emotional than men are. This is possibly one reason God entrusted the leadership of the church to men.

We notice also that Paul is extremely hard-line with those who don't want to work (2 Thessalonians 3:6-13), as well as with those who are critical and divisive (Titus 3:9-11). In a tense situation, men tend to withdraw (stop working), while women tend to manipulate and take over the leadership from the withdrawn brother, which does not bring about the spiritual balance that God commands. Women who do take over leadership do not like Paul and his no-nonsense approach as to how the church should be governed. (And critical and divisive women, or men, certainly do not appreciate Paul's challenge to them...unless they truly have a heart for God and want to change.)

Far from having a poor evaluation of women, Paul understands them—and men—all too well! Paul was neither a woman-hater nor a man-hater; he was, however, a sin-hater. We must realize that

Paul's insight is not his own; it is *God's* insight into our characters. God's word is true, on target and always penetrating.

How About a Retrial?

Paul did not misunderstand women, but women have misunderstood Paul—and all the more as amazingly, few have read what he actually said. We have found that good-hearted women—those who are really serious about giving God control of their lives and "crucifying the sinful nature"—are not the ones who stumble on Paul's teaching. Rather, the women who fight against Paul are the ones who tend to be critical, emotional and rebellious.

Why the Confusion?

We do not deny that women were misunderstood or oppressed in Jesus' day. They certainly were, and this has been the case in every generation.[3] Treatment of women isn't much better today: in many Third World countries women are worked like slaves, and in developed countries they are treated as sex objects, misunderstood by men too selfish to listen and really care. In any and every society the position of women would be radically improved if men—and women—would put the principles of God's word into practice.

All men and women share in the same mission: to spread the word of God to a world without love (Matthew 28). As long as we keep that straight, we will have true unity between sexes. Gratitude and sincere appreciation for hard work (1 Thessalonians 5:12) will replace critical attitudes and competitive feelings.

Instead of reading what the Bible really says, most women have listened to their friends' ill-informed opinions about the Bible's oppression of women and Paul the "woman-hater." Uncritically they have swallowed these negative attitudes hook, line and sinker. Sadly, many people are looking for issues to campaign against. They simply would not have time for this if they were about their mission—if they could say, with the apostle Paul, that they are being "poured out" for the cause of Christ (2 Timothy 4:6).

The massive confusion results from *ignorance* and *selfishness.* Only when men and women make time to study God's word and deny themselves (Luke 9:23) will we be united in our purpose and find what we were striving for all along: meaning and happiness in life.

Notes

[1] Sirach 22:3. See also 25:13-26:18.

[2] In "democratic" India, which is more than eighty percent Hindu, opportunities for its half a billion women are limited indeed. Hinduism teaches that you get in this life what you earned in the last; a certain fatalism and passivity are not, therefore, entirely unexpected. Wife-beating and spousal abuse are rampant. A disgrace in the history of India is *suttee* (the burning alive of a Hindu widow on her husband's pyre).

With their official "one-child policy," Chinese authorities often force women to abort or "terminate" the newborn and exact heavy fines from persons exceeding the one-child limit. China is officially atheist, though Taoism-Buddhism survives in many parts. Until the Revolution of 1911, women's feet were commonly "bound" (wrapped so tightly that they became grossly deformed, useless for walking).

Female circumcision is an international issue. Such nations as Chad, Somalia and the Sudan show unspeakable cruelty toward their female citizens in continuing this barbaric ritual, first recorded in Egypt more than four thousand years ago. Much of Muslim or tribal Africa enforces this rite of passage.

[3] Contemporary sociology recognizes the abysmal status and treatment of women in the ancient world and the utter contrast in which the Christian religion held out true hope to women. In *The Rise of Christianity,* (Princeton University Press, 1996), page 118, sociologist Rodney Stark writes:

> Both Plato [*Republic* 5 (1941 ed.)] and Aristotle [*Politics* 2, 7 (1986 ed.)] recommended infanticide as legitimate state policy. The Twelve Tables—the earliest known Roman legal code, written about 450 BC—permitted a father to expose any female infant and any deformed or weak male infant (Gorman 1982:25). During recent excavations of a villa in the port city of Ashkelon, Lawrence E. Stager and his colleagues made a gruesome discovery in the sewer that ran under the bathhouse. "This sewer had been clogged with refuse sometime in the sixth century AD. When we excavated and dry-sieved the desiccated sewage, we found [the] bones...of nearly one hundred little babies apparently murdered and thrown into the sewer (1991:47)." Examination of the bones revealed them to be newborns, probably day-olds (Smith and Kahila, 1991).

3
Reexamining the Biblical Doctrine of Hell

One disciple wrote me this question:

> "I remember that in one of your books (I think it might have been *The Spirit*), you made passing reference to the fact that hell will not be a place of eternal torment, as some understand it, but rather of permanent destruction. I wonder if you could explain that a little bit more for me? I've never studied the issue in depth, but I've always had an impression that hell involved unending suffering, rather than oblivion."

Hell is both dreadful and irreversible. In the new *Shining Like Stars*, you will find an entire study on judgment in chapter 13. This might be a good place to begin your own study.

As for ultimate "extinction" instead of *infinite* torment, you should be aware that Christians are divided on the proper understanding of the nature of the punishment of the wicked in the world to come. Though a case can be made for either side of the debate, it is my understanding that punishment comes to an end at some point (Luke 12:47-48, the passage about "many blows" and "few blows"). Whether this is after days or years—or even millions of years—I have no clue and prefer not to speculate. Be advised that in my capacity as writer, I do not claim to speak "for the movement." I am sharing my convictions—with which you are welcome to disagree! The following is a paper I have written on this subject.

Heaven and Hell
Terminal Punishment

—Fall 2000 (original version 1992)

In my view *hell doesn't last infinitely,* but instead destroys the individual after an appropriate length of time. Therefore, hell is eternal in its consequences, not in its duration. This is in contrast to the traditional view, which holds that the individual is tormented endlessly in the fire of hell. In other words, God prolongs one's life infinitely for the purpose of punishment. Perhaps we'd do better to adopt the term "terminal punishment" in describing this new view. Any length of time in hell less than infinite implies the terminal view.[1]

If you conceive of eternal punishment as lasting millions and millions of years, you are in basic agreement with my thesis. Even five hundred million years, as long as that may seem, is virtually nothing in comparison with infinite time. Any amount of time less than forever (infinity) implies the terminal view, as the following table illustrates.[2]

Time and Eternity

Time in Hell	View of Punishment
One million years	Terminal
One week	Terminal
One year	Terminal
Ten days	Terminal
One second	Terminal
Eight and one-half minutes	Terminal
Two years	Terminal
Five hundred billion years	Terminal
Four hours	Terminal
Seven trillion years	Terminal
Seven trillion centuries	Terminal
Seven trillion millennia	Terminal
Ten googol[3] years	Terminal
Infinite time	Traditional

Hopefully, the difference between traditional and terminal understandings is now clear. The terminal view is simply that after a period of torment ("corporal punishment") suited to the individual, God destroys him or her ("capital punishment"). The distinction can also be understood by the following paradigm:

Paradigms of Punishment

Traditional view:	Corporal punishment (forever)
Annihilationist view:	Capital punishment
Terminal view:	Corporal and capital punishment

In addition to terminal punishment, I also hold that *the soul of man is not eternal.* Therefore, immortality is a gift only for the saved. These two doctrines—the mortality of the soul and the finite nature of hell—are central to the terminal view of hell, especially since the development of this article in the early '90s.

The Right Attitude

I realize many disciples sincerely hold to the traditional position, while a number have been persuaded to the terminal view. Currently, there's no consensus, though a show of hands might result in the triumph of the traditional view. But truth isn't determined by a show of hands or by popular referendum; what's needed is a thorough study of the issue. We need to study what the inspired word of God says (and it says quite a lot!).

My aim was never a movement-wide pronouncement on the subject (Acts 15-style), but rather a diligent search into the truth of the matter. The issue isn't what feels right or what works best, but what the truth is. I hope the paper is helpful to you as you study the matter for yourself.

Objections Considered

Let's be a little unorthodox and consider some of the objections before we even develop the thesis. This is helpful because of the emotionally loaded nature of any discussion on eternal punishment. Preconceptions eventually need to be addressed. (For example, as long as the person you are talking with has "the sinner's prayer" or "the thief on the cross" in the back of his mind as an objection to getting baptized, you'll be limited in your ability to persuade him to do so. Show him there's another feasible interpretation, and his mind opens up to the possibility.) The question is, "Is it even possible to consider another view of hell?"

Jesus' Words in Mark 9

What about Jesus' own words on hell? Jesus is in fact the Bible's main spokesman on the subject. Do his words refute the terminal view, or is there another reasonable way to look at the subject?

> "If your hand causes you to sin, cut it off. It is better for you to enter life maimed than with two hands to go into hell, where the fire never goes out. And if your foot causes you to sin, cut it off. It is better for you to enter life crippled than to have two feet and be thrown into hell. And if your eye causes you to sin, pluck it out. It is better for you to enter the kingdom of God with one eye than to have two eyes and be thrown into hell, where
>
> "'their worm does not die,
>   and the fire is not quenched.'
>
> Everyone will be salted with fire." (Mark 9:43-49)

Mark 9 seems to imply that the wicked will forever burn in the fire of hell. Similarly, John 3:16 seems to support salvation by faith alone. After all, it states that "whoever believes in him" will not perish. But then Luke 13:5, supplying additional information, shows that we must repent in order not to perish. Surprisingly, a closer look at Mark 9 hardly proves that the wicked burn forever and ever. The passage doesn't explicitly say that people in hell are undying. The only "immortal" creatures in the passage are the worms! And anyway, an eternal fire wouldn't logically necessitate that whatever is thrown into it would burn eternally, only that the fire itself wouldn't go out. Whatever is thrown into that fire would sooner or later be completely burned up. It's a *consuming* fire.[4] Let's carefully consider the Isaiah passage that Jesus cites:

> "...all mankind will come and bow down before me," says the LORD. "And they will go out and look upon the dead bodies of those who rebelled against me; their worm will not die, nor will their fire be quenched, and they will become loathsome to all mankind." (Isaiah 66:23-24)

What does this passage, borrowed by Jesus to illustrate the nature of hell, really teach?

- The bodies are dead, not living. They're unconscious.
- They are those who rebelled against God.
- They are being consumed by worms and fire.
- The scene evokes feelings of disgust, not pity.

Whether we should take the immortality of the worms literally is certainly questionable. But the thrust of the passage is clear enough: the rebels have been destroyed. They aren't conscious. They feel no pain. Furthermore, the emotional panorama is different to the one conjured up by the traditional view. The sight is disgusting. No feelings of pity are welling up—only loathing and disgust. After all, they're dead and decaying.

Has Jesus perhaps changed the original meaning of the Isaiah passage? The burden of proof is on the traditional view, which Isaiah 66 and Mark 9, naturally read, do not convincingly support. There certainly seems to be a case for the terminal view here. I'm not asking you to accept the new view just yet, only to admit that the objection from Mark 9 isn't conclusive. Isaiah 66 may very well speak against the traditional view.

We may assume that everyone in Jesus' day understood him to mean *infinite* torment; but the support for this is weaker than we may think. It comes primarily from the Apocrypha. The first time the Apocrypha (c. 200 BC-100 AD) speaks of eternal torment is in the book of Judith, written approximately 125 BC:

> Woe to the nations that rise up against my people! The Lord Almighty will take vengeance on them in the day of judgment; fire and worms he will give to their flesh; they shall weep in pain forever. (Judith 16:17)

Whereas Isaiah's fire and worms destroy the individual, Judith's fire and worms torture. What a contrast! This is the one clear passage in support of the traditional view from the Apocrypha.

Other apocryphal passages on the subject support the view that the wicked will be destroyed, *not* tormented forever. Even the later *Pseudepigrapha* has a mixed witness on this subject, some passages in favor of the later view, others favoring the traditional view. The Dead Sea Scrolls, from the two centuries before Christ, unanimously teach the extinction of the wicked.

To be fair, admittedly, some Patristic writers (church fathers in the first few centuries after Christ) do follow Judith. However, we must remember that (1) their writings date from after the close of the New Testament canon; (2) Jesus gives no credence to the (OT) apocryphal writings; and (3) these books lack Biblical authority, since we can hardly decide our views based on extra-Biblical sources.

The Meaning of 'Eternal' in Matthew 25:46

If it can be shown that "eternal" is used in more than one way, then there's a case for the terminal view. But *can* it in fact be taken in only one way? The familiar conclusion to the Parable of the Sheep and the Goats reads, "Then they will go away to eternal punishment, but the righteous to eternal life." At first inspection the passage seems to support the traditional view strongly. The reasoning is simple: if the eternal life lasts forever, then the eternal punishment must last equally long. Therefore hell is forever—settled! And this does sound logical.

The following chart details some of the Biblical words related to the concept of eternity.

Word	Language	Definition
Aion	Greek	Age (*aeon*); segment or period of time.
Aionios	Greek	Lasting, eternal, relating to an *aion*.
Aevum	Latin	Age, lifetime, eternity.
Aeternus	Latin	Lasting, eternal.
olam	Hebrew	Nominally: world, age Adjectivally: everlasting, perpetual...

Alas, there are good reasons to reject this interpretation. To begin with, it doesn't fit very well with Mark 9, if our analysis above is correct. The first passage assumes that consciousness has ceased; the other, it is alleged, assumes consciousness is unending. Therefore, there's a logic problem. Why would someone be tortured *forever* in hell for sins committed during a limited period of time on earth? Looking at the Bible's own commentary on the unchanging character of God (Malachi 3:6), we see that God rewards to the thousandth generation, but punishes only to the third or fourth (Exodus 20:5-6). But the most important argument against the traditional view of Matthew 25 is the evidence from Jude.

> In a similar way, Sodom and Gomorrah and the surrounding towns gave themselves up to sexual immorality and perversion. They serve as an example of those who suffer the punishment of eternal fire. (Jude 7)

Go back to Genesis 19, or go to the geographical area of Sodom and Gomorrah. Did the combustion continue after the fire and brimstone fell? Is it still burning today? So, how exactly were they "an example of those who suffer the punishment of *eternal* fire"? (emphasis added). Is Jude confused? (And was Peter confused in 2 Peter 2:6?)

Actually, in the Scriptures, Sodom and Gomorrah are the prototype of those who suffer God's wrath and punishment:

- Genesis 19:24-29
- Deuteronomy 29:22-24
- Isaiah 1:9, 13:19-22
- Jeremiah 49:18, 50:40
- Lamentations 4:6
- Amos 4:11
- Zephaniah 2:9
- Luke 17:28-29
- 2 Peter 2:6

Yet in every one of these cases, as with the original (Sodom), the punishment is limited in duration.

Now back to the question of the meaning of "eternal" in Matthew 25:46. How could hell be eternal *without* lasting forever? It could be eternal in its effects. The result of punishment is total, irreversible, eternal. In eternity the verdict will forever read the same. Before reacting against this interpretation of the word "eternal" as special pleading, consider several passages that are apropos.

Hebrews 6:2 speaks of "eternal judgment." Is the process of judging itself eternal, or only the consequence, the sentence? It's obvious that in this verse "eternal" is being used to describe the effects, not the act of judging itself. Incidentally, eternal judgment, which is the subject of this paper, is one of the "elementary teachings"—all the more reason to figure this out!

Mark 3:29 mentions an "eternal sin." Its guilt will never be forgiven. But it isn't the sin itself (as an action) that's eternal. The sin isn't committed forever and ever, but the results of the sin are everlasting. It will never be forgiven.

Hebrews 9:12 speaks of the "eternal redemption" that Christ has effected. Hebrews, of all the NT books, makes it clear that the redeeming itself is a once-for-all event. So, we're speaking of the results or consequences of the redemption Jesus Christ has purchased for us. His atoning death is over; now he is resurrected and at the right hand of the Father.

What can we conclude from these three passages?

- In all three cases the word "eternal" is *not* used in the usual, more familiar way. So, "eternal" can be understood in more than one way.
- In Matthew 25:46 there's no compelling reason to take "eternal" in the traditional way. The language and interpretational possibilities don't demand it.
- Jude 7 supports the terminal view against the traditional view.

Matthew 25 by no means forces us to accept the traditional view. We must allow the Bible to define its terms. In the case of the word "eternal," we must determine whether Biblical writers and speakers mean eternal in the sense of a "continuous action or state," or eternal in the sense of a "consequence or result."[5]

Revelation 14 and 20

Before I tackle a few objections from Revelation, let me encourage us to exercise caution when interpreting this highly figurative "book of prophecy" (Revelation 22:19). Many false doctrines have been fabricated from its verses, and we need to tread carefully.

In my view it's impossible to take this book literally. However, by "literally" I don't mean "seriously" or "at face value." The book must be taken seriously, as both warnings and blessings are attached to reading it in chapters 1 and 22. But actually, much of the

Bible is impossible to take "literally," for example: apocalyptic, a good deal of prophecy, many figures of speech, accommodative language, psalms and other kinds of poetry. The rule of thumb when reading Revelation is: *Take the passage figuratively unless forced to do otherwise.* Literal interpretation almost always does violence to this text. (For example, the 144,000 in heaven of Revelation 7 and 14, who, strictly speaking, are celibate Jewish males only!)

Revelation has immediate application to the Roman Empire, which was just commencing its severe persecution of the Christians in the reign of Domitian, the Caesar from 81-96 AD. In Revelation 22:14 we read of people both inside and outside the city, but from 22:11 and 22:2 it's quite clear there were still many non-Christians (those "outside") carrying on life as normal. This is after the New Jerusalem has come down! This is in contrast to the common view that takes the book, especially its final chapters, to describe some future state. There's a lot we can glean from Revelation, yet we must glean ever so carefully.[6]

There are two passages problematic for the terminal view. If they're taken at face value, there are certainly some questions to answer.

> A third angel followed them and said in a loud voice: "If anyone worships the beast and his image and receives his mark on the forehead or on the hand, he, too, will drink of the wine of God's fury, which has been poured full strength into the cup of his wrath. He will be tormented with burning sulfur in the presence of the holy angels and of the Lamb. And the smoke of their torment rises for ever and ever. There is no rest day or night for those who worship the beast and his image, or for anyone who receives the mark of his name." (Revelation 14:9-11)

While a cursory reading might lead you to think that this ongoing torment is for all eternity, there are several reasons to discount this interpretation. The passage is specific to the time of the Roman Empire, and the language is highly figurative. The smoke is eternal, but not explicitly the torment, which may be our conclusion, but the passage doesn't state it. "No rest day or night" may just as well imply a limited period of time as an eternal one.

Revelation 18:18 and 19:3 are especially helpful:

> When they see the smoke of her burning, they will exclaim, "Was there ever a city like this great city?" (Revelation 18:18)

> And again they shouted:
> "Hallelujah!
> The smoke from her goes up for ever and ever."
> (Revelation 19:3)

These passages describe the destruction of Rome, imperial headquarters of the persecuting power and enemy of the faithful. Notice the words "for ever and ever," which emphasize not the duration of the smoke or burning, but the permanence of the destruction. The careful reader will note that the "smoke of her burning" (18:9) is the result of her being "consumed by fire" (18:8), the just punishment for her sin (18:6-7). In this case, punishment was proportional and finite, not infinite in duration.

This has OT parallels. Isaiah 34:10 speaks of the destruction of Edom: "It will not be quenched night and day; its smoke will rise for ever." Edom was laid waste centuries before Christ, and the smoke can *only* be taken in a figurative way. Since this can't be taken literally, and neither can Revelation 19:3, there seems little reason to take Revelation 14:11 literally either. As for the drinking of the wine of God's fury, an OT prophetic verse, from an oracle against Edom, sheds further light on the interpretation of Revelation 14:

> Just as you drank on my holy hill,
>   so all the nations will drink continually;
> they will drink and drink
>   and be as if they had never been.
> (Obadiah 1:16)

The implication is that they drink themselves into oblivion, into nothingness. Then there's the second problematic verse, this time from chapter 20:

> And the devil, who deceived them, was thrown into the lake of burning sulfur, where the beast and the false prophet had been thrown. They will be tormented day and night for ever and ever. (Revelation 20:10)

Since 20:15 says the *lost* will be thrown into the lake of fire, it is argued, their torment must also last for ever and ever. But can we safely move from the destruction of a beast and a false prophet and the devil to the destruction of sinners in hell, taking for granted that they are analogous?

The beast and the false prophet are *corporate entities*. They represent Rome, the civil power, and Rome, the religious power. Can a government or a religion be tortured in fire? Not literally. Again, 20:15 doesn't explicitly say that sinners' torment is for ever and ever. Yet even if it did, I doubt such a figurative book as Revelation would be able to settle the fundamental question conclusively.

Death and Hades will also be destroyed in the fire, according to Revelation 20:14, but what does that mean except that they will come to an end? As in the case of the beast and the false prophet, it's difficult to conclude anything definite about the fate of sinners from this. The one very definite piece of information we do have is the following:

> ...and each person was judged according to what he had done....The lake of fire is the second death. If anyone's name was not found written in the book of life, he was thrown into the lake of fire. (Revelation 20:13, 15)

Could "the second death" be the final extinction of the individual? The first death is simply the death we'll all experience, unless Jesus returns while we're still alive. It's normal, physical death. The second death, on the other hand, is the destruction mentioned in Matthew 10:28. There's no life, no consciousness, nothing at all after the second death. Isn't this the natural reading of the passage?

The OT allusion in Revelation 20 is to Psalm 140:9-10. Let's take a look at Psalm 140 so we can be sure we are understanding Revelation correctly:

> Let the heads of those who surround me
>   be covered with the trouble their lips have
>   caused.
> Let burning coals fall upon them;
>   may they be thrown into the fire,
>   into miry pits, never to rise. (Psalm 140:9-10)

"The trouble their lips have caused" implies that the punishment will fit, or be in proportion to, the crime. The limit is determined by the amount or nature of the "trouble" caused. Obviously the "trouble" isn't infinite, so it is unwarranted to assume the pain of the fire is infinite. This is the OT background of Revelation 20.[7] Thus we see that Revelation 20:10, which discusses the fate of the devil, cannot be used to prove the duration in hell of the punishment of unforgiven sinners. Let's close the discussion of Revelation by returning to one of the final verses:

> And if anyone takes words away from this book of prophecy, God will take away from him his share in the tree of life and in the holy city, which are described in this book. (Revelation 22:19)

The tree of life gave immortality, according to the Genesis account. Here we see that even true Christians can *lose* their immortality, which is a God-given blessing, if they tamper with the word of God. But if the traditional view is right, it's impossible for anyone to lose his immortality, which is considered innate and automatic.

We can therefore conclude that neither of the problematic verses in Revelation conclusively teaches that people will be tortured forever in hell. It simply isn't there.

Summary: Initial Objections

I've taken all this time to answer the most common objections in order to show that the terminal view is a viable interpretation. Though the bulk of the positive evidence for this view is forthcoming, it will be nowhere near as persuasive to someone who has already made up his mind on the interpretational possibilities.

We saw that Jesus' words in Mark 9, often presumed to back the traditional view, actually strongly support the terminal view. Matthew 25, on the other hand, though seeming at first to support the traditional view (and without other passages to clarify it, appears to do so decisively), is inconclusive because of the ambiguity of "eternal." There are good reasons to understand "eternal" in the second, also Biblically common, sense. This fits in excellently with Jesus' words in Matthew 10:28: "Rather, be afraid of the One who can destroy both soul and body in hell."

Revelation, interpreted by many to support the traditional view incontrovertibly, does nothing of the kind. Revelation 14 draws on OT imagery where the image of eternal burning cannot possibly be construed to be "eternal" in the literal, traditional sense. The same can be said of Revelation 20.

The traditional view, if it is true, must base itself on clear, nonambiguous passages of Scripture. However, the most compelling passages marshaled to support it are all somewhere between ambiguous and detrimental to the view.

The Terminal Position on Heaven and Hell

The terminal view finds support in both Old and New Testaments. Both contain the same teaching about the Judgment Day, the mortality of the soul, heaven as the reward for the righteous, and hell culminating in annihilation as the punishment for the wicked.

Support from the Old Testament

There will be a Judgment Day. This may not come as a shock to most readers, but just to set the record straight, let's review the Biblical teaching in the Old Testament.

> Whatever is has already been,
>   and what will be has been before;
>   and God will call the past to account.
>
> I thought in my heart,
>
> "God will bring to judgment
>   both the righteous and the wicked,
> for there will be a time for every activity,
>   a time for every deed." (Ecclesiastes 3:15, 17)

Since not all right is rewarded nor all wrongs righted here in the earthly life, God will take care of things afterward. Judgment Day involves a review of all actions, to be carried out when the time is right. See also Ecclesiastes 11:9.

> Now all has been heard;
>   here is the conclusion of the matter:
> Fear God and keep his commandments,
>   for this is the whole duty of man.
> For God will bring every deed into judgment,

including every hidden thing,
whether it is good or evil. (Ecclesiastes 12:13-14)

...Will he not repay each person according to what
he has done? (Proverbs 24:12)

This last verse is the one Paul uses in his discussion of judgment in Romans 2:6. He appeals to the authority of the Old Testament, as NT writers constantly did.

One thing God has spoken,
    two things have I heard:
that you, O God, are strong,
    and that you, O Lord, are loving.
Surely you will reward each person
    according to what he has done.
(Psalm 62:11-12)

These things you have done and I kept silent;
    you thought I was altogether like you.
But I will rebuke you
    and accuse you to your face. (Psalm 50:21)

Exactly when will this rebuke occur? The storms of life (Matthew 7:25) don't always do the trick, and it seems God is keeping silent for the time being. But he *will* speak, and there will be many surprised people at the judgment (Psalm 73:17). Their face-to-face rebuke is pending. (Further evidence comes from Proverbs 11:19, 21, 23.)

Thus we see that the Old Testament teaches a time of judgment, with subsequent reward or punishment, in accordance with one's deeds. Moreover, this teaching isn't limited to the Wisdom literature or the prayers of the psalmists. Just like the New Testament, the Old Testament teaches a comprehensive judgment (Genesis 18:25, Deuteronomy 32:35-36, Hebrews 10:30, Romans 12:19).

The Mortality of the Soul

Man is Mortal. The doctrine of man's mortality is well established in the Old Testament, but the traditional or orthodox view is that the human soul is eternal. The Scriptures, however, do not contain the doctrine of the immortal soul—there's no verse to turn to on this.

Often it's said that OT writers taught man's mortality (i.e., no "eternal life") because of their limited knowledge about the afterlife. There's another possibility, however—that the immortality of the soul is a false assumption, unsupported by the Bible. The lack of support in the Old Testament in this case doesn't need to be explained away; it's to be expected.

The surprising thing is that the Old Testament isn't simply silent on the subject. There's a definite "Old Testament" teaching. I put that in quotation marks because it's not really only an OT teaching; it's a Bible teaching. (In the same way, it would be misleading to say that God's goodness is an OT teaching, since the New Testament teaches exactly the same.) The real question is, "What does the Bible teach?"

In the Old Testament we read of *Sheol* as the abode of the dead, rendered "hell" in older translations. Yet in modern English translations we do not find the word "hell" anywhere in the Old Testament. For instance, the NIV variously translates it as "the grace" or "Death," but indicates *Sheol* in the footnotes. This shouldn't be taken to mean that hell is only a NT concept. Quite the contrary. Let us return to Psalm 140:

> Let the heads of those who surround me
> be covered with the trouble their lips
> have caused.
> Let burning coals fall upon them;
> may they be thrown into the fire,
> into miry pits, never to rise. (Psalm 140:9-10)

The wicked will be thrown into the fire. They will be swallowed up. They will be "consumed." The lake of fire is an OT teaching. (Revelation 20 appropriately borrows and adapts this feature in its description of the punishment of the wicked, particularly the opponents of the Christians in the Roman Empire. These enemies of the faith were also slanderous persecutors, just like David's enemies in Psalm 140:11.) [8]

Eternity in Heaven for the Saved

The saved will be with God in heaven eternally. According to the Old Testament, we'll be with God "for ever and ever," enjoying "eternal pleasures at [his] right hand" (Psalm 21:4, 16:11). Nor is there any hint that the reward is restricted to a limited period of time.

> Therefore my heart is glad and my tongue rejoices;
>   my body also will rest secure,
> because you will not abandon me to the grave,
>   nor will you let your Holy One see decay.
> You have made known to me the path of life;
>   you will fill me with joy in your presence,
>   with eternal pleasures at your right hand.
> (Psalm 16:9-11)

> And I—in righteousness I will see your face;
>   when I awake, I will be satisfied with seeing your
>   likeness. (Psalm 17:15)

While it is true that the notion of heaven was not developed in the OT period, it would be false to claim heaven is exclusively a NT concept.

Punishment by Fire for the Lost

The wicked will be punished with fire. As with the previous doctrine, the punishment of the wicked by fire is not as elaborately or explicitly taught in the Old Testament as in the New Testament, but once again, it is clearly intimated. Psalm 21:9, which appears in the next subsection, is one example of a "fire" passage, as is the following: "Fire goes before him and consumes his foes on every side" (Psalm 97:3).

Or take this passage from the prophets:

> See, the Name of the LORD comes from afar,
>   with burning anger and dense clouds of smoke;
> his lips are full of wrath,
>   and his tongue is a consuming fire.
> His breath is like a rushing torrent,
>   rising up to the neck.
> He shakes the nations in the sieve of destruction;
>   he places in the jaws of the peoples
>   a bit that leads them astray.
> And you will sing
>   as on the night you celebrate a holy festival;
> your hearts will rejoice
>   as when people go up with flutes

to the mountain of the LORD,
    to the Rock of Israel.
The LORD will cause men to hear his majestic voice
    and will make them see his arm coming down
with raging anger and consuming fire,
    with cloudburst, thunderstorm and hail.
The voice of the LORD will shatter Assyria;
    with his scepter he will strike them down.
Every stroke the LORD lays on them
    with his punishing rod
will be to the music of tambourines and harps,
    as he fights them in battle with the blows
        of his arm.
Topheth has long been prepared;
    it has been made ready for the king.
Its fire pit has been made deep and wide,
    with an abundance of fire and wood;
the breath of the LORD,
    like a stream of burning sulfur,
    sets it ablaze. (Isaiah 30:27-33)

Fire is the most common metaphor for judgment and punishment in the Bible, and the Old Testament is no exception.

Destruction in Hell, Not Eternal Torment

The wicked will be destroyed, not just tormented forever. If this proposition is true, then either we must rely upon the New Testament alone for the concept of unending conscious torment or admit that the traditional view is the product of human theology. This in itself wouldn't be surprising, considering the many doctrines that began to be spawned at the very time the New Testament was being written. The issue, however, must be settled from the Bible itself.

Your hand will lay hold on all your enemies;
    your right hand will seize your foes.
At the time of your appearing
    you will make them like a fiery furnace.
In his wrath the LORD will swallow them up,
    and his fire will consume them. (Psalm 21:8-9)

This portion of Scripture says that the wicked will be *consumed*. When you consume your dinner, what's left? Nothing! (See also

Psalm 59:13.) How long does the consumption last? Until they are no more. The effect, however, is eternal; there isn't the slightest chance of it ever being reversed. They will cease to *exist*.

> Those who are far from you will perish;
>   you destroy all who are unfaithful to you.
> (Psalm 73:27)

> The senseless man does not know,
>   fools do not understand,
> that though the wicked spring up like grass
>   and all evildoers flourish,
> they will be forever destroyed. (Psalm 92:6-7)

> The wicked man will see and be vexed,
>   he will gnash his teeth and waste away;
>   the longings of the wicked will come to
>   nothing. (Psalm 112:10)

Notice the progression in this last Psalm. The wicked man proceeds along this path:

Being Vexed⟶Gnashing Teeth⟶Wasting Away

In the Bible, gnashing of teeth is a sign of anger, not agony. The wicked man doesn't gnash his teeth forever; he ultimately wastes away. We've been conditioned to think of gnashing of teeth as the involuntary response of souls in torment, whereas actually, it is the proud and angry response of those who refuse to humble themselves before God! In Psalm 37 it isn't possible to take "gnashing" as a pitiful act of agonized torture. Here it's the proud and willful expression of scorn by a wicked person toward the good:

> The wicked plot against the righteous
>   and gnash their teeth at them;
> but the LORD laughs at the wicked,
>   for he knows their day is coming.
> (Psalm 37:12-13)

Taking the verse in context, the gnashing is going on *before* Judgment Day. The common understanding of gnashing as a response to torment is incorrect. Remember how the Jews gnashed their teeth at Stephen before stoning him (Acts 7:54).

The destruction of the wicked follows from another Biblical principle, namely that God's wrath runs it course (Isaiah 57:16 and Psalm 103:9). Although it could last infinitely long, if that were God's will, the Scriptures show that his punitive action in hell is limited in duration. There's logically a limit to God's anger—logically, because the punishment for sin is always in proportion to the sin itself. A finite quantity of sin doesn't require an infinite amount of punishment.

One final comment on the destruction of the wicked: Spiritual death isn't the same as physical death. The wages of sin is physical death, according to Romans 5. Through Adam, sin and death entered the world. But there's a further kind of death: spiritual death. (In one sense, of course, as non-Christians we were dead spiritually [Ephesians 2], but this is in a figurative sense.)

The spirit of man dies when God destroys both soul and body in hell (Matthew 10:28). Sooner or later, all men die physically. But to perish spiritually (Luke 13:5)—this is a much more frightful thing. The point is that, just as physical death means the end of life in the physical body, so spiritual death means the end of life as spiritual beings. We are all created as spiritual beings, so when our spiritual lives end, we cease to exist.

You may also want to consult these verses on the ultimate destruction of the wicked: Psalm 9:5, 37:20, 37:37-38, 68:2, 104:35; Proverbs 12:7, 21:28 and 24:19-20.

Before you study *closely* the OT teaching about the afterlife, it may seem the Old Testament is silent about heaven, hell and the traditionally accepted Christian picture. In fact, it is not silent. It only seems silent because it gives no support to the accepted view. The Old Testament, once again, isn't silent about the end of the wicked. It's only silent as to the view we'd expected to find!

Before moving on to the NT teachings, let me state one of the most surprising conclusions I've come to in my study: *The Old Testament and the New Testament teach substantially the same about heaven and hell.* The Old Testament and the New Testament are in perfect harmony. This is encouraging because it shows the organic unity and harmony of the Scriptures. Remember, the Old Testament was the Bible for the early Christians. It isn't hard to see how they would have been able to teach accurately about the afterlife using only the Old Testament.

Do you wonder why I cite Psalms so often? Because the teaching on the subject is so clear there. Certainly, we must be careful in using the Psalms in doctrinal discussions and recognize when poetic forms of speech are being used. But the wise use of exegetical tools can reveal many crucial ideas. (Incidentally, Psalms is the *most* quoted book in the New Testament, followed by Isaiah and Deuteronomy.) It should come as no shock that the psalmists write often of the future of the wicked and the future of the righteous. These writers frequently pondered the future and expressed their firm faith and hope in God's justice, which meant two things: *punishment* for the wicked and *reward* for the righteous. There's no hint that this punishment is infinite. Rather, it's finite, or terminal.

Support from the New Testament

Most of us are so much more familiar with the NT teaching on these matters that fewer verses are needed to substantiate the basic points than for the discussion of the Old Testament and afterlife. Jesus reaffirmed the OT doctrine of the day of judgment. (See also Matthew 25.)

> "Do not be amazed at this, for a time is coming when all who are in their graves will hear his voice and come out—those who have done good will rise to live, and those who have done evil will rise to be condemned." (John 5:28-29)

Purgatory is ruled out of court, as it lacks any supporting scripture. The New Testament teaches but two alternatives.

The Mortality of the Soul

Man is mortal; immortality is a gift. The NT teaching of the mortality of the soul is identical to the OT teaching, a consistent thread of doctrine from Genesis onward.

> "For just as the Father raises the dead and gives them life, even so the Son gives life to whom he is pleased to give it." (John 5:21)

> "...you reject it and do not consider yourselves worthy of eternal life, we now turn to the Gentiles."
> ...When the Gentiles heard this, they were glad

> and honored the word of the Lord; and all who were appointed for eternal life believed. (Acts 13:46, 48)

> To those who by persistence in doing good seek glory, honor and immortality, he will give eternal life. (Romans 2:7)

Now we must admit that these are difficult verses to understand if we were born immortal! *Eternal life is conditional (not for everybody) and positive.* If we were innately immortal, then immortality wouldn't be conditional. And if one can be immortal in hell then, for most of humanity, immortality is the greatest imaginable curse. In the Bible immortality is presented as a blessing:

> For the wages of sin is death, but the gift of God is eternal life in Christ Jesus our Lord. (Romans 6:23)

> I declare to you, brothers, that flesh and blood cannot inherit the kingdom of God, nor does the perishable inherit the imperishable....For the perishable must clothe itself with the imperishable, and the mortal with immortality. (1 Corinthians 15:50, 53)

Mortality *can* yield to immortality. This is awesome! But is it an automatic change happening to every human soul at judgment, regardless of his or her spiritual standing before God? Not at all. This inheriting of immortality is a positive thing, sung to the tune of victory:

> When the perishable has been clothed with the imperishable, and the mortal with immortality, then the saying that is written will come true: "Death has been swallowed up in victory." (1 Corinthians 15:54)

> ...the hope of eternal life, which God, who does not lie, promised before the beginning of time.... (Titus 1:2)

Now if this is our *hope* (eternal life), do we possess it innately, whether or not we follow Christ? Romans 8 and some clear thinking elucidate the matter. "...But hope that is seen is no hope at all. Who hopes for what he already has?" (Romans 8:24).

If we already had eternal life, we wouldn't need to hope for it. Yet, not until the last trumpet will eternal life unconditionally be ours. Eternal life is a reward for the saved—and for the saved only. This is also the teaching of Jude and Revelation: "Keep yourselves in God's love as you wait for the mercy of our Lord Jesus Christ to bring you to eternal life" (Jude 21).

Yes, we begin to receive eternal life in baptism, but in another sense, the victory isn't clenched till we've died faithful. By that time it's impossible to fall away and forfeit the enormous gift we've received. Eternal life will be our reward. "And if anyone takes words away from this book of prophecy, God will take away from him his share in the tree of life…" (Revelation 22:19).

It is indeed possible to lose our share in the tree of life. If this happened, we would certainly not live forever. Once again, check it out in Genesis: "'…[The man] must not be allowed to reach out his hand and take also from the tree of life and eat, and live forever'" (Genesis 3:22).

Just as in the Old Testament, the New Testament teaches immortality is a reward from God, a reward only for the faithful. The traditional idea of *unending conscious torment and innate immortality* is severely at odds with the Bible.

Incidentally, several early writers affirmed the eternal torment view: Justin, Jerome and Augustine, to mention a few of the big names. Yet, several of the early "church fathers" also advocated infant baptism and apocryphal writings—even the priesthood. The point is that regardless of what leading intellectuals taught, the Bible and the Bible only is authoritative in settling Biblical questions.

Eternity in Heaven for the Saved

The saved will be with God in heaven. You knew this already, but just to be encouraging: "…And so we will be with the Lord forever" (1 Thessalonians 4:17). No one contests this, the supporting Scriptures are ample, and this paper is really a new view of hell, not heaven,[9] so let's move on!

Punishment by Fire for the Lost

The wicked will be punished with fire. The OT teaching is repeated in the New Testament: "But for those who are self-seeking and reject the truth and follow evil, there will be wrath and anger"

(Romans 2:8). What kind of wrath and anger? In Mark 9, Jesus, much to the chagrin of modern "churchianity" and its professional clergy, speaks at length about hell.

> "If your hand causes you to sin, cut it off. It is better for you to enter life maimed than with two hands to go into hell, where the fire never goes out. And if your foot causes you to sin, cut it off. It is better for you to enter life crippled than to have two feet and be thrown into hell. And if your eye causes you to sin, pluck it out. It is better for you to enter the kingdom of God with one eye than to have two eyes and be thrown into hell, where
>
> " 'their worm does not die,
>   and the fire is not quenched.'
>
> Everyone will be salted with fire." (Mark 9:43-49)

Like the Old Testament, the New Testament says the wicked are thrown into the fire. Interestingly, only Jesus and his brother James *explicitly* mention the burning fire of "Gehenna" (hell). Paul never explicitly mentions it, yet he gave the leaders of the church at Ephesus the "full counsel" (Acts 20:27). Draw your own conclusion. Before we discuss the fire's duration, let's move on to the final element in New Testament teaching on the afterlife.

Destruction in Hell, Not Eternal Torment

The punishment ends in destruction. In Luke 13:5 we read that unless we repent, we will all "perish." But what does it mean to "perish"? In its basic use, the word carries no sense at all of continued existence or consciousness. The Latin word *perire,* which gives us our English word "perish," means "to pass away, come to nothing, lose one's life." The Oxford English Dictionary gives this definition: "To come to an untimely end; to suffer destruction; to lose its life." An end implies nothing further; destruction means annihilation; loss of life precludes eternal life. We know what the word "perish" means, but our understanding of Luke 13 has been determined by the Catholic church, not by standard English usage. In fact, the definition of "perish" changed in late Middle English (around 1300). The later, modified meaning, according to the Oxford entry, was: "To incur spiritual death; to suffer moral ruin." But this isn't the original meaning of the word, which was redefined by the medieval church. We are all too familiar with the confusion caused by the later definition of the word *baptisma* (baptism)!

Try to set aside the traditional view, at least for the time being. Ask Dante to wait outside the door till we've finished scouring the New Testament. Let's begin in Matthew.

> "Enter through the narrow gate. For wide is the gate and broad is the road that leads to destruction, and many enter through it." (Matthew 7:13)

Where does the broad road lead? To eternal torment? No, to *destruction*. This is more like the unthinking buffalo herd stampeding over the edge of the cliff than the masses falling into the hands of Lucifer's torturers. The Hebrew writer concurs:

> If we deliberately keep on sinning after we have received the knowledge of the truth, no sacrifice for sins is left, but only a fearful expectation of judgment and of raging fire that will consume the enemies of God. (Hebrews 10:26-27)

The fire of God's wrath ("raging") will totally *consume* God's enemies. This requires some time. Consumption may be slow, or it may be fast, but it isn't instantaneous.

Jesus himself described opposite destinies in Luke 16. The rich man wasn't yet consumed. To illustrate, if acid *consumes* an object, how much is left? None of it, if it's really consumed and not just corroded. Consumption is total by definition. It's the same with eating. Once you consume your food, it's gone. Chew, swallow, digest—but once you've done that—it's gone. Again, the Hebrew writer mentions destruction:

> But we are not of those who shrink back and are destroyed, but of those who believe and are saved. (Hebrews 10:39)

If we shrink, back we'll be punished. But the truth is that we'll also be *destroyed*. The passage says nothing of a sort of "figurative" destruction. Destruction is destruction.

> Then death and Hades were thrown into the lake
> of fire. The lake of fire is the second death. If
> anyone's name was not found written in the book
> of life, he was thrown into the lake of fire.
> (Revelation 20:14-15)

To understand the "second" death, begin by asking what the first one is. Of course, it's physical death. The second one is the spiritual capital punishment administered by God: "'...Rather, be afraid of the One who can destroy both soul and body in hell'" (Matthew 10:28).

God can *destroy* our souls. This passage isn't talking about Satan. He himself is one of those who will be cast into hell (Revelation 20:10). When God destroys a soul, there will be nothing left. After that point, the soul will no more survive than the physical body will survive. The soul of man is most emphatically *not* eternal: "if he condemned the cities of Sodom and Gomorrah by burning them to ashes, and made them an example of what is going to happen to the ungodly..." (2 Peter 2:6).

What is going to happen to the ungodly? They are going to go to hell. The punishment of hell is not under dispute. Hell is Biblical, real and horrible. The issue is, What is the nature of the punishment? And this passage says that Sodom and Gomorrah, which were burnt to ashes, are an example of what will happen to the ungodly. So if the traditional view is correct, why aren't these cities still burning?

> ...They are like brute beasts, creatures of instinct,
> born only to be caught and destroyed, and like
> beasts they too will perish. (2 Peter 2:12)

> By the same word the present heavens and earth
> are reserved for fire, being kept for the day of judg-
> ment and destruction of ungodly men. (2 Peter 3:7)

Destruction is the order of the day, not eternal, conscious torment. Yet some will experience a longer punishment than others will, as Luke 12 makes clear:

> "That servant who knows his master's will and does
> not get ready or does not do what his master wants

will be beaten with many blows. But the one who does not know and does things deserving punishment will be beaten with few blows. From everyone who has been given much, much will be demanded; and from the one who has been entrusted with much, much more will be asked." (Luke 12:47-48)

Responsibility is proportional, and judgment is based on ability and knowledge. This isn't just logical—it's Biblical!

Jesus' analogy makes an assumption about time. If it should be taken literally, some were going to receive more blows than others. Which takes longer, few blows or many? Many, of course. In other words, some punishments will last longer than others. That's the implication of the text. So the length of the punishment is proportional to the amount of guilt or the level of responsibility the individual failed to live up to.

Another implication is that the punishment will eventually end. This means that whether it is either a million years or forever—however hard psychologically for us to grasp—does actually make a difference. We are not splitting hairs here. In mathematics class, students are not allowed to "round up" really large numbers to infinity! The difference, in fact, between any number, however large, and infinity is *infinity!* One is limited, the other is infinite. This is precisely the point of this article: The punishment of hell runs its course.[10]

Both Old Testament and New Testament teach the same: a punishment for the wicked that begins in torment and ends in destruction. Once again, consider the paradigm laid out at the beginning of the article.

Paradigms of Punishment

Traditional view:	Corporal punishment (forever)
Annihilationist view:	Capital punishment
Terminal view:	Corporal and capital punishment

Related Questions

Many protests have been leveled against this view, and they are not to be taken lightly. As Proverbs 18:17 says, "The first to present his case seems right, till another comes forward and questions him." A good theory must be able to stand the test of criticism. Yet are the objections really weighty enough to support the traditional view and overthrow this one? We shall see.

The Source of the Traditional View

If the new view is right, why didn't Jesus ever correct the traditional view? Quite simply because the "traditional" view may not have become widely accepted until well after Jesus' time. We've assumed Jesus supported the traditional view through default. (He never tried to correct the common misunderstanding.) But what makes us so sure first century Jews held to eternal punishment in the traditional sense?

They didn't get the idea from the Old Testament. Neither the Old Testament nor the New Testament teaches eternal torment. Like me, you probably thought it was somewhere in there, right? (Which verse? I haven't been able to find it.) Plato, four centuries earlier, had taught the immortality of the soul, but his influence was little felt in NT times. And the first time the Apocrypha, written shortly before and after the first century, speaks of eternal torment is Judith 16:17. So where did Jesus' contemporaries supposedly get the view of infinite hell?

Moreover, are we sure there was a consensus in Jesus' day? Why would Jesus have attempted to correct the prevailing view if there *was* no unified view in his day? Similarly, it would certainly be misleading to claim that there's only one view on the afterlife in today's religious world!

Yet even if the majority of Jews in Jesus' day *did* believe in the later Catholic view, and even if, for his own reasons, Jesus made no attempt to enlighten them, this is irrelevant as far as we're concerned. The question about hell is a Biblical question, and its answer needs to be derived, ultimately, from the Bible. Speculation about Jesus' reasons for addressing or for not addressing the various conceptions in his day are bound to be highly speculative.

Luke 16

The account in Luke 15 of the Rich Man and Lazarus turns out to not be much of an objection, since the passage never says the rich man would be in the fire of hell forever. It merely says that "those who want to go from here to you cannot, nor can anyone cross over from there to us" (Luke 16:26). We only assume he would be there forever. I've preached it, and many have shuddered to think of their loved ones in hell "for eternity," but the traditional torment interpretation has been read into the text, which, honestly, allows either view.

Galatians 1:9

The Greek words *anathema esto,* strictly speaking, do not read, "let him be eternally condemned," but rather, "let him be 'anathema.'" Anathema is the strongest possible curse, but no hint of eternal torment is inherent in the Greek. The New International Version translators have opted for a more traditional translation of the Greek expression, which is fine, provided we haven't determined in advance what "eternally condemned" means.

Remember, eternal condemnation doesn't necessarily mean eternal torment, as we have seen, but rather an eternal sentence from which there will never be escape or appeal. So, this is not a case of mistranslation. As in the instance of Luke 16, we see how easy it is to read our position into the text. We read "eternally condemned" and think, "See, it says *eternally* condemned. Hell is eternal!" Well, hell *is* eternal, but that's not the question. The question is what "eternal" means in this context and what "eternal condemnation" means in the Bible.

If the verse had said, "Let him be eternally *tormented,*" we would have a case for the traditional view. But it doesn't, and so we don't. Moreover, Galatians 6 teaches the opposite of the traditional view anyway:

> The one who sows to please his sinful nature, from that nature will reap destruction; the one who sows to please the Spirit, from the Spirit will reap eternal life. (Galatians 6:8)

Destruction is the end of the wicked, not eternal torment.

Matthew 5 and 18

> "I tell you the truth, you will not get out until you have paid the last penny." (Matthew 5:26)

> "In anger his master turned him over to the jail-
> ers to be tortured, until he should pay back all he
> owed.
> "This is how my heavenly Father will treat each
> of you unless you forgive your brother from your
> heart." (Matthew 18:34-35)

Let's begin by honestly admitting that these passages are difficult to
understand. Jesus could certainly mean that we *never* "pay" our
way out and thus remain in hell forever. On the other hand, he
could also mean that we sooner or later *do* pay our way out. The
passages allow either interpretation. But they absolutely do not prove
the traditional view because they do not prove either view.

Luke 12

Luke 12:57 says some will receive few blows, some many blows.
Its application to hell seems clear and direct. Yet it has been ob-
jected that the proper context of Luke 12:47-48 rules out applying
the principle to non-Christians. Take a look at the passage again:

> "That servant who knows his master's will and does
> not get ready or does not do what his master wants
> will be beaten with many blows. But the one who
> does not know and does things deserving punish-
> ment will be beaten with few blows. From everyone
> who has been given much, much will be demanded;
> and from the one who has been entrusted with
> much, much more will be asked." (Luke 12:47-48)

Peter had asked in verse 41, "'Lord, are you telling this parable
[about his return in judgment] to us, or to everyone?'" In fact, Jesus
gave no direct answer to the question, instead discussing the mas-
ter-servant relationship. Still, the passage does seem to apply to
God's people more than to outsiders. But will God's delinquent
people really be "beaten"? What about "no condemnation" in Christ
(Romans 8:1)? And even if they were beaten (which in my mind is
questionable theologically), then how much more would the principle suit non-Christians! Moreover, the passage distinguishes between servants who know their master's will and those who don't.
But don't all *Christians* essentially "know" their master's will? Those

who know less, like non-Christians, are those "who do not know" (see also 2 Thessalonians 1:8).

The principle here concerns knowledge and responsibility. Since this pertains to God's way of dealing with men, it seems unlikely that he would suspend the principle in the case of non-Christians. So while we can accept that the passage was originally spoken to the Twelve and applies to the servant people of God, it's untrue that the principle is invalid for the lost in general.

Daniel's Three Friends

> ...the fire had not harmed their bodies, nor was a hair of their heads singed; their robes were not scorched, and there was no smell of fire on them. (Daniel 3:27)

Daniel 3:27 too has been taken to illustrate or prove that God can keep sinners in the fire eternally. "See, the fire didn't kill them!" it is pointed out. "The fire didn't destroy them—their physical bodies were somehow preserved." Yet by strict logic, this is actually an instance of God's *protection* from burning, hence a poor choice for the traditional view.

Once again, it's not disputed that God can do whatever he wants to. "Our God is in heaven; he does whatever pleases him" (Psalm 115:3). The point isn't what God *can* do, but what he does. Thus Shadrach, Meshach and Abednego are of no assistance in our investigation.

What About the Burning Bush?

> There the angel of the LORD appeared to him in flames of fire from within a bush. Moses saw that though the bush was on fire it did not burn up. (Exodus 3:2)

Does this passage prove that lost souls burn forever in hell? Naturally, God has the ability to cause something to burn without burning up. Conceded! He's God, after all. But in this case the bush's burning was only temporary. Its combustion was assisted and prolonged by God, but not eternally—only in accordance with God's purposes.

Final Appeal

Well, the first has presented his case, and the second has as well (Proverbs 18:17). How forceful do the objections seem to you now? I want to leave you with three questions:

1. Are you dissuaded from the terminal view because it takes more than one Bible scripture to explain the duration of hell? This is the case for many Bible teachings. To convincingly explain baptism or Jesus' divinity, it's helpful to use a number of verses. Do you think all this is exegetical gymnastics, or is it sound?

2. What does *the Bible*—not your minister, small group leader, church, Bible commentary or even your conscience or feelings—say about the subject? The Bible is our only arbiter and authority in settling the issue.

3. Is the alternative, the traditional view of hell/immortality of the soul, really more convincing than the view here presented?

Of course you must do your own homework, as a Berean of noble character (Acts 17:11). Re-read the paper; check the Scriptures in context; think it through. Make your own decision.

Finally, what will be different if we embrace this new understanding of judgment and hell? A number of things, but let's start with what will stay the same.

What Is the Same?

- Hell is still real, horrible, consciously experienced and irreversible.
- We aren't becoming "annihilationists," nor are we giving up the very clear Biblical teaching of the raging fire which consumes the enemies of God.
- We still sentence ourselves by sin, failure to seek God and rejecting the Savior.
- Evangelism is still imperative; no one goes to heaven apart from Jesus.
- We'll still have many enemies and detractors who'll scoff at the concept of an authoritative and sovereign God who punishes.

What Is Different?

- No one will spend eternity (infinitely) in hell. Punishment eventually *terminates* in destruction.
- Eternal life is a precious gift from God, not an automatic.
- The Old Testament and the New Testament square with each other.
- Many Christians will be relieved and enjoy the Christian life more than ever.

Check your heart. Don't let your feelings stop you from accepting this view, but on the other hand, don't let your feelings draw you into this view. Some of the implications are attractive, but we can't go around deciding doctrine based on our feelings.

My appeal to you, brothers and sisters, is to study the topic for yourself, without rushing to a hasty conclusion or embracing this teaching because it appeals to you personally. Base your conclusion on Biblical grounds first and foremost. Then we will be able to:

> ...leave the elementary teachings about Christ and go on to maturity, not laying again the foundation of repentance from acts that lead to death, and of faith in God, instruction about baptisms, the laying on of hands, the resurrection of the dead, and eternal judgment. And God permitting, we will do so. (Hebrews 6:1-3)

Notes

[1] This article is the fifth version of my article on heaven and hell. In the first version (spring 1992), I called the new position on hell "temporary punishment." The term however was misleading. The Bible certainly teaches that the punishment of hell is eternal, and no one will "graduate" from hell to heaven. The question is, "What is meant by 'eternal'?" The next edition still focused too much on the implications of the new view and consistency with the justice of God, which clouded the issues and made the discussion too emotional. Frank input from a number of thinkers, especially Doug Arthur, Gordon Ferguson, Marty Wooten, Mike Fontenot, Roger Lamb and Kip McKean (as well as various world sector leaders) has helped me enormously. In following versions, I cut back to a bare bones presentation of the view.

[2] I admit that in the next world (in what we call eternity), we may be entering a timeless state that defies chronological analysis.

[3] A "googol" is defined by mathematicians as 10^{100}, which is one followed by 100 zeroes. There is also a *googolplex,* which is ten raised to the power of a googol!

⁴ To illustrate, the "unquenchable fire" of Jeremiah 17:27 does *not* burn forever, though the destruction it wreaks is certainly serious and thorough.

⁵ In addition, there are a number of scriptures in which words such as "forever," "eternal" and "everlasting" do not necessarily entail a sense of *infinite* duration. For example, the following list is based (only) on the Greek root *aion* which appears in the LXX and the New Testament numerous times, with the general sense of "(world) age, forever, always, eternity, etc." In none of the following cases does the word *aion* bear the sense of infinite eternity.

Genesis 6:4—men of old (giants/ungodly persons/fallen ones/sons of Cain) did not live infinitely.

Jeremiah 25:12—destruction of Babylon (though not literally destroyed)

Genesis 9:12—perpetual generations

Exodus 21:6—the man or woman would become one's servant "for ever" (KJV)

Leviticus 25:34—perpetual possession of fields

Deuteronomy 23:3—"forever" is parallel to the tenth generation (KJV)

1 Samuel 1:22—young Samuel was to serve at the house of the Lord "for ever" (KJV)

1 Chronicles 16:15—"forever" is parallel to 1000 generations—also Psalm 105:8

Ezra 4:15, 19—Israelites had been "eternally" resisting political domination.

Psalm 24:7—"ancient" doors

Proverbs 22:28—"ancient" boundary stone

Jonah 2:6—prophet confined in the fish "forever"

⁶ For a few good reading suggestions on Revelation, see Jim McGuiggan, *The Book of Revelation* (Lubbock: Montex, 1978); Gordon Ferguson, *Mine Eyes Have Seen the Glory: The Victory of the Lamb in the Book of Revelation* (Woburn, Mass.: DPI, 1996); and Ray Summers, *Worthy Is the Lamb* (Nashville: Broadman Press, 1951).

⁷ Remember, the Old Testament is the key for understanding Revelation. In 404 verses, there are more than 500 OT references and allusions. That's why I always recommend people read the whole Old Testament before coming to any hard and fast conclusions about the last book of the Bible.

⁸ Just as the doctrine of the mortality of the soul has not found wide acceptance within Christendom, so it is within Islam. Interestingly, the Qur'an too seems to allow for an end to the torment of the wicked in hell.

As to the duration of heaven and hell, all Muslims agree that the state of bliss in heaven is eternal. The Qur'an itself assures believers of the eternality of heaven (3.198, 4.57, 25.15, 50.34). But there is no unanimous agreement as to the duration of the lost in hell. The Qur'an speaks of the punishment and torment of eternity, and describes the fire and hell itself as eternal (10.52, 32.14, 41.28, 43.74). The majority of orthodox Muslims accept the eternality of hell based on this testimony. On the other hand, based on such passages as 78.23, 11.107 and 6.128, which indicate the damned will remain in fire for a long time or will be there as long as God wills, many contemporary Muslims believe that the Qur'an leaves open the possibility that the punishment of hell will not last forever. (Normal L. Geisler and Abdul Sareeb, *Answering Islam: The Crescent in the Light of the Cross* [Grand Rapids: Baker, 1993], 57.

⁹ Since the first edition of this paper, my understanding of what happens after death has changed substantially. I teach that for the saved, after death we proceed directly to paradise. Not until the return of Christ and our resurrection will we go to heaven. For more on this, see my *The God Who Dared*, Appendix E, "What Is Paradise?" (DPI, 1997).

¹⁰ I don't have any guesses about how long hell lasts for different people. This would be a matter of speculation.

4
The Apocrypha

One of my online readers recently wrote:
> "What are the specific reasons (e.g. Scriptural contradictions) that we can cite from Scripture or other sources that show that the Apocrypha is not inspired by the Holy Spirit?"

Another reader wrote:
> "While speaking with a Catholic priest recently, I challenged him on the fact that we cannot add extra books (i.e. Apocrypha) into the Bible hundreds of years later as we choose to. He said that the Greek translation of the Old Testament (the Septuagint) which the NT writers quoted from contained the Apocrypha as well as the usual OT books. I think this is correct and was wondering how to reply to this."

The books of the Apocrypha were written in the centuries between the testaments—after the Old Testament was completed, and for the most part, before the time of the New Testament. While some of these writings contain valuable historical information, others are not trustworthy sources. In some places, they contradict the Bible, advocating such doctrines as penance, purgatory, almsgiving for forgiveness, sex for procreation only, prayers to and for the dead, and a host of other un-Biblical notions. During the Catholic Counter-Reformation, the Apocrypha, which had been familiar to believers for 1,500 or more years, were given full canonical recognition. This is why Catholic Bibles have had six extra complete books, plus additions to several other Biblical books, inserted into the Old Testament. The books of the Apocrypha are never directly quoted in the Bible, and there is no evidence that Jesus recognized them as authoritative. Their inclusion in the sixteenth century elevation to canonical status is fully understandable only in light of highly questionable sixteenth century church politics. Earlier this year I carried out a special study on the Apocrypha, and I would like to share it with you. I would encourage you to read the Apocrypha for yourself. In the process I believe you will gain more understanding of why most Christians through the ages have refused to accept their inspiration.

As we begin a closer look at the Apocrypha, you may find it useful to peruse the list of terms below.

Terminology

Apocrypha—In the broader sense, the noncanonical literature; in the narrower sense, the additional books (and portions of books) interspersed throughout the Old Testament. Literally, Greek for "hidden things."

Apocryphon—The singular of *apocrypha*.

Canon—Literally, the "measure" or yardstick; the officially accepted list of the books of the Bible.

Council of Trent—The Roman Catholic Council (1545-1563) at which issues raised by the Protestant Reformation were considered, as Catholicism fortified its position.

Counter-Reformation—The Catholic reaction to the Protestant Reformation.

Deuterocanonical—Of a second order of inspiration or canon, as opposed to "protocanonical" (like the word "Deuteronomy," or "second giving of the law").

DSS—The Dead Sea Scrolls

LXX—Roman numerals for "seventy," the supposed number of translators of the Septuagint in the third century BC. LXX represents the Greek Septuagint translation of Old Testament and Apocrypha made in Egypt for the Jews there who spoke Greek better than Hebrew. (See question 1 under Various & Sundry.)

Patristics—Study of the writings of the early church fathers, principally from the late first to the late fourth centuries AD.

Pseudepigrapha—Writings of false or pseudonymous authorship. All the OT Apocrypha are anonymous (no authorship is attributed in the work itself) or pseudonymous (work is falsely attributed to another Biblical writer) except for Sirach, and yet properly speaking, the Pseudepigrapha are works which appear outside the official OT Apocrypha.

Qumran—The monastic community in ancient Israel which preserved the Dead Sea Scrolls which were found in 1947.

Reformation—The Protestant movement against the moral and doctrinal corruption of the medieval Catholic church. Though rooted in the work of reformers in the fourteenth and fifteenth centuries, Luther is generally credited with having launched the Reformation in 1517.

Septuagint—The Greek translation of the OT Scriptures made by Egyptian Jews of the third to second centuries BC; the Bible of the Greek-speaking Christians. From *septuaginta,* Latin for "seventy." See "LXX," above.

Vulgate—The common ("vulgar") Latin language translation of the Old Testament, Apocrypha and New Testament undertaken by Jerome in Bethlehem around the year 400.

The Apocrypha: Second Thoughts

Perhaps you have heard of Tobit, Judith or Ecclesiasticus. Maybe you have even read the Wisdom of Solomon or 1 and 2 Maccabees. You may know that Catholic and Orthodox Bibles contain extra verses in such books as Daniel and Esther. In my experience, few ministers of the gospel have ever taken the trouble to read the Apocrypha (a plural noun)—and yet they have many opinions about them! As Alexander Pope said, "A little learning is a dang'rous thing/ Drink deep, or touch not the Pierian spring."

This study has been prepared for the benefit of those who minister to the churches that they may (1) have an accurate knowledge of these works and (2) be stimulated to study the books themselves. In addition, this article has been written for our brothers and sisters in Sweden, where the Apocrypha are included in most modern Bibles.

General

Most of the apocryphal books of the Old Testament were produced between 200 BC and 100 AD. To fully appreciate these often misunderstood writings, we must realize that the Jews did not have a rigorous doctrine of inspiration worked out. It is difficult, if not impossible, to prove that the Jews some two millennia ago viewed all their writings as on the same level of inspiration. They did not read the Scriptures in a book, all neatly authenticated as divinely inspired and bound together. They read from scrolls.

At the core of their Scriptures was the Torah, the books of the Law handed down by Moses. The next circle included the Prophets, which called people back to the Torah, and finally come the writings. It is outside this third "concentric circle" that we find the many apocryphal writings. (See figure A below.) There is a substantial difference between the canonical writings and the apocryphal writings, and this difference lies in whether or not the writings are true. *Although the apocryphal books do contain many lofty thoughts and interesting stories, they often contradict known facts of Biblical history and sound Biblical principles.*

Figure A

Were these books at some time meant to be included in the Biblical canon? Should Christians read them? Has there been some sort of conspiracy or cover-up? After all, *apocrypha* in Greek means "hidden things," though in no sense have the apocryphal writings been "hidden" from anyone.

The apocryphal books, including all the works which appear between the covers of the Bibles of the various factions of Christianity, can be grouped into eighteen documents, with a total equivalent of nearly two hundred chapters—roughly the length of the Qur'an or eighty percent of the length of the New Testament. For your convenience, they are listed below. In addition, at the end of this study you will find a short glossary of some of the terms which will frequently appear.

Old Testament Apocryphal Documents

Apocryphal Book	Chapter Numbers
1 Esdras	1-9
2 Esdras	1-16
*Tobit**	1-14
Judith	1-16
Additions to Esther	11-16 (Latin), 10-11 (Greek)
Wisdom of Solomon	1-19
Sirach (Ecclesiasticus)	1-51
Baruch	1-5
Letter of Jeremiah	6 (= Baruch 6)
Song of the Three	3 (between Daniel 3:23 and 3:24)
Susanna	13 (= Daniel 13)
Bel and the Dragon	14 (= Daniel 14 in Latin; added to Daniel 12 in Greek)
Prayer of Manasseh	1
1 Maccabees	16
2 Maccabees	15
3 Maccabees	7
4 Maccabees	18
Psalm 151	1

*Titles in italics appear in standard Roman Catholic Bibles.

Reconsidering

In 1985 I scoured the Catholic Apocrypha and published an article in a London church bulletin. A year or two later, I put out a second version of this article. I taught, as most Protestants and independents do, that these books were *added* to the Roman Catholic canon—albeit with "deuterocanonical" (second-order canon) status—

during the Counter-Reformation. Whether I realized it or not at the time, my conclusions were fundamentally the same as those of most scholars outside the Catholic or Orthodox camp. In 1991, I continued my study, fitting the new information I learned into the same mindset. I even published an online piece in my regular *Bible on Trial* column in early 2000 in which I stated that these books were added into the Bible in the sixteenth century. Now I have reconsidered.

In 2000, I carefully re-read the apocryphal books, including those normally included in Orthodox Bibles, with or without official canonical status. My conclusion that these extra works are not inspired by God remains unchanged; however, I feel I was unfair in my previous handling of some of the texts, in quoting them without sufficient regard to their context.

Moreover, it is now my view that the Catholics did not truly add these books to their Bible at the Council of Trent on April 8, 1546. Rather, Protestant reformers (like Erasmus), in their "housecleaning" zeal, aimed to subtract them from the Bibles and worship of the day. And by the nineteenth century, they had finally succeeded.

Earlier this year I read through several medieval manuscripts of the Bible at Duke University's Rare Book and Manuscript collection. Particularly striking was a thirteenth century Latin Vulgate Old Testament which was copied in France. All of the Catholic "extra books," including 1 and 2 Esdras, were present. Later I examined a fourteenth century Bible at the University of Michigan's fabulous collection in Ann Arbor. Same observation! In other words, the extra books were already in Bibles—long before the Reformation.

In response to the attacks of the reformers, the Catholics "upgraded" the Apocrypha to full inspired status. In the fourth session of the Council of Trent, they decreed of the Apocrypha,

> If anyone does not receive these entire books, with all their parts, as they are accustomed to be read in the Catholic Church and are found in the ancient edition of the Latin Vulgate, as sacred and canonical, let him be anathema.

Yet, though the reformers assigned the Apocrypha only secondary status (they were "deuterocanonical," to use the emerging term), they did include them in their new Bible translations. While they could not bring themselves to consider these works "inspired," neither could they bring themselves to remove them from their churches. In other words, by the sixteenth century, the apocryphal books, for all intents and purposes, had come to enjoy a position of favor and inspiration in the eyes of the Catholic Church.

Patristics

How did I come to these conclusions? To begin with, in addition to re-reading all of the Old Testament Apocrypha, I checked every patristic reference to the Apocrypha in the first three centuries of Christianity. (The term "patristics" refers to the writings by Christian thinkers from the late first century to the fourth century.) I noticed that there are only a few citations in the first half of the second century, yet a huge number in the second half of that century. The third century sees even more references, and the same is true of the fourth. The patristic writers routinely and consistently quote apocryphal works *as Scripture.* See for yourself if you doubt this; I am confident you will come to no other conclusion.[1]

Two things struck me. First, by the mid-second century the majority of the patristic writers accepted the inspiration of the Apocrypha. Since they lived so much closer to the first century, I wondered in my heart whether perhaps it was *we* who got it wrong. That is, I was willing, at the beginning of my study, to consider whether I had rejected the Apocrypha without sufficient evidence.

Second—and this is very important—it would be false to say that writers from the late first to mid-second century viewed the Apocrypha as inspired. There are only three or four quotations to that effect, hardly enough on which to build a doctrine of inspiration. And yet, despite the concerns of some fourth century clerics about the Apocrypha (like Jerome), the books were included in the influential Latin Vulgate translation.

To sum up, the Patristics show us an evolving view of the Apocrypha, which had matured by mid-second century—three or four generations after the NT books were written and with plenty of time for a wrongheaded understanding to develop. From the third century on, the Apocrypha were especially cherished by the Christian church, despite some controversy in the fourth century about their true status.

Relation to the New Testament

Significantly, there are no direct quotations from the Apocrypha in the New Testament, though there would seem to be many allusions (e.g. Wisdom 13:5, 13:8, 14:24 and 14:27 in Romans 1:20-29; Wisdom 12:12, 12:20 and 15:7 in Romans 9:20-23; Wisdom 9:15 in 2 Corinthians 5:1 and 5:4; Wisdom 7:22-26 in Hebrews 1:1-3; 2 Maccabees 6:18-7:42 in Hebrews 11:34-35; Sirach 5:11 in James 1:19; Sirach 15:11-12 in James 1:13, etc.). Considering that the New Testament quotes the Old Testament over and over again—in addition to the hundreds or possibly thousands of allusions—it is highly suggestive that no one can produce a single convincing NT quotation of an OT apocryphal verse. In short, it does not appear that the NT writers (apostles of Jesus and their immediate disciples) considered these books inspired by God.

The Pseudepigrapha

In this article, I am not going to take up the curious case of Jude's direct quotation of 1 Enoch, as this is not part of the OT Apocrypha proper—1 Enoch is part of the OT *Pseudepigrapha*, literally "works of false authorship." These include the Apocalypse of Abraham, the Apocalypse of Adam, the Testament of Adam, the Life of Adam and Eve, Ahiqar, the Letter of Aristeas, Aristeas the Exegete, Aristobulus, Artapanus, 2-4 Baruch, Cleodemus Malchus, the Apocalypse of Daniel, (noncanonical) Psalms of David, Demetrius the Chronographer, Eldad and Modad, the Apocalypse of Elijah, 1-3 Enoch, Eupolemus, Pseudo-Eupolemus, the Apocryphon of Ezekiel, Ezekiel the Tragedian, 4 Ezra, the Greek Apocalypse of Ezra, Questions of Ezra, Revelation of Ezra, Vision of Ezra, Fragments of Pseudo-Greek poets, Pseudo-Hecataeus, Hellenistic Synagogal Prayers, the Martyrdom and Ascension of Isaiah, the Ladder of Jacob, Prayer of Jacob, Jannes and Jambres, Testament of Job, Joseph and Aseneth, History of Joseph, Prayer of Joseph, Jubilees, 3-4 Maccabees, the Prayer of Manasseh, Syriac Menander, the Testament of Moses, Orphica, Philo the Epic Poet, Pseudo-Philo, Pseudo-Phocylides, the Lives of the Prophets, History of the Rechabites, Apocalypse of Sedrach, the Treatise of Shem, the Sibylline Oracles, Psalms of Solomon, Testament of Solomon, Theodotus, Testaments of the Three

Patriarchs, Testaments of the Twelve Patriarchs, and the Apocalypse of Zephaniah. To read these documents, see *The Old Testament Pseudepigrapha, Volumes 1 and 2.*[2]

Therefore, when people ask why the Apocrypha were "excluded" from the canon, they seem to be totally unaware that such an enormous body of religious literature was written by the ancient Jews. The real question is, "Why are the canonical books in the Bible?"[3]

Let me offer an analogy. You are trying to explain your faith to a nonbeliever, and you happen to walk into a Christian bookstore, showing him the Bible section. "Are all these other books inspired, too?" he asks you. "No, only the Bibles," you reply. How odd it would be if he asked you why the thousands of other books "never made it into the Bible." In the same way, there are major differences between the canonical books and all the (many) other religious writings.

The English Bible

Wyclif, who translated the Bible into (Middle) English in the late 1300s, included the apocryphal works (except for 2 Esdras), though with a caveat that they "shall be set among apocrypha, that is, without authority of belief" ("shal be set among apocrifa, that is, with outen autorite of bileue"). Wyclif worked from the Latin Vulgate, which includes nearly all the Apocrypha. Note that the earliest English Bibles excluding the Apocrypha appeared only in 1599. And in 1615 the Archbishop of Canterbury made it a crime punishable by one year in prison to produce a Bible without the apocryphal books.

The earliest editions of the King James Version (oddly considered "inspired" by many English speakers worldwide), were completed in 1611 and included the Apocrypha. The first King James Version without it appeared only in 1629, though most editions continued to include the Apocrypha. In 1827 Protestant publishers of the English Bible generally stopped printing these books, though they were (and are) still read in churches. Apocryphal themes and stories have had a profound influence on literature, music and art, which explains the reluctance of many to abandon them as inspired writings.

Book by Book

In the next section we will touch lightly on each book of the Apocrypha, noting strong and weak points, truth and error. As you will see when you read the Apocrypha for yourself, some sections are awesome; others awful. It certainly is the mixture of error and truth which is problematic for those who insist on the inspiration of these books.

1 Esdras

- The historical book of 1 Esdras, consisting of nearly unchanged excerpts from the LXX of Chronicles-Ezra-Nehemiah, is also called 3 Esdras in the Vulgate.
- It is the apocryphal book most intimately connected with the Old Testament.
- Its aim is to emphasize the contributions of Josiah, Zerubbabel and Ezra to the reform of Israelite worship.
- Despite its historical value, there are many minor discrepancies with the canonical OT accounts. For example, see 5:73.
- Since the Council of Trent (1545-1563), it has usually appeared in an appendix after the New Testament.

2 Esdras

- The apocalyptic work (the same genre as Revelation) of 2 Esdras consists of seven revelations coming through the mediation of the archangel Uriel.
- Like 1 Esdras, since Trent it has been placed in an appendix as "4 Esdras."
- Chapters 3-14 are considered to have been written in the late first century by a Jewish author.
- Chapters 1-2 are considered to have been written in the second century AD, and chapters 15-16 in the third century AD. Chapters 1-2 and 15-16 are missing in all Eastern versions.
- The central concern is theodicy (the justice of God and the problem of suffering).
- Interestingly, 3:36 teaches that although all the pagan nations are lost, there are some individual Gentiles who are obedient to God's commandments.
- Six-sevenths of the earth is land, 6:42 teaches, and only one-seventh is water. (In actuality, more than three-quarters of

the earth's surface is covered with water.) Moreover, in 16:58, 2 Esdras teaches that the earth is suspended over the waters.

- Quite interesting for understanding first century expectations, 7:28 begins a highly messianic section. Chapters 13-14 equate the Messiah with the Son of God. (This may explain Jesus' preference for the more neutral term, "Son of Man," which is found in Ezekiel and Daniel.)

- The efficacy of prayers for the dead is explicitly *denied* in 7:36ff. For this reason, the Roman church cut out this section (compare with 2 Maccabees 12:43-45, which affirms the value of prayers for the dead). Similarly, 7:105 allows no intercession for the wicked on the day of judgment.

- The first sacrifice was offered when the world was three thousand years old, according to 10:45. And yet the Old Testament never once attempts to provide a picture of the age of the earth.

- In 14:44, 2 Esdras says that ninety-four books have been revealed. This would include the twenty-four canonical OT books (remembering that several books were combined into one, such as The Twelve, which we divide into the Minor Prophets) and another seventy esoteric (apocryphal) works.

Tobit

- The short story of Tobit was one of the most popular books among the Jews. It is interesting and enjoyable reading.

- Tobit and Judith (next work) were placed between Nehemiah and Esther.

- In 1:8 we see that Tobit gave not just a tithe, but *three-tenths.*

- There are some historical inaccuracies, such as in 1:15. Another error is in 14:15, an anachronism based on confusion among names which was common in the Judaism of "Tobit's" day.

- In 4:15 we find the "Silver Rule" or "negative Golden Rule." And yet Tobit is not portrayed as a stingy person. In 4:16 Tobit teaches his son, Tobias, to "Give all your surplus to charity." There are many passages in the Apocrypha that insist on the power of almsgiving, such as Tobit 12:9: "For almsgiving delivers from death, and it will purge away every sin."

- The practice of offering food to the dead is apparently approved in 4:17.
- In 6:6-8 we find blatant superstition:

> Then the young man said to the angel, "Brother Azarias, of what use is the liver and heart and gall of the fish?" He replied, "As for the heart and the liver, if a demon or evil spirit gives trouble to anyone, you make a smoke from these before the man or woman, and that person will never be troubled again. And as for the gall, anoint with it a man who has white films in his eyes, and he will be cured."

Two observations here: Jesus never followed this advice; and exorcism is totally absent from the Old Testament, even though the pagan nations surrounding Israel were controlled by their fear of demons. Again, in 8:3 we find that a demon is repulsed by an offensive odor.

- In 14:4 the prophecy of Jonah about the destruction of Nineveh is still to be fulfilled. And yet Nineveh is in the wrong location geographically. (Even the Greek historian Xenophon [c. 400 BC] didn't know its location.) The guess was inaccurate.

Judith

- Judith is another popular folk tale about a pious and beautiful woman who saves her people.
- As is common with the Apocrypha, we find errors in its history. In 1:1-6 the Babylonian king, Nebuchadnezzar, is placed *after* the exile.
- In the final chapter, we read about a hell of infinite conscious torment.

> Woe to the nations that rise up against my people! The Lord will take vengeance on them in the day of judgment; fire and worms he will give to their flesh; they shall weep in pain forever. (16:17)

This is significant because it is a misunderstanding of the fire and worms of Isaiah 66:24. They do not eternally torment their victims; they consume insentient corpses. The same doctrine is taught in Sirach 7:17 and 4 Maccabees 9:9. And yet it is not at all certain that Jesus endorsed the apocryphal view of hell.

Additions to Esther

- Interspersed throughout the canonical Esther are 107 extra verses.
- The main purpose seems to be to add a religious element. (God does not explicitly appear in the canonical Esther.)

Wisdom of Solomon

- The Wisdom of Solomon is also called "the Book of Wisdom" or simply "Wisdom."
- Composed in the first century BC, this Greek book was quite possibly originally written in Hebrew.
- A phenomenal messianic passage is found in 2:12-3:9.
- Despite the great wisdom of this book (no sarcasm intended), there are some theological problems. In 14:9 we read, "For equally hateful to God are the ungodly man and his ungodliness."
- Interestingly, in 18:13 Israel is "God's son," just as in the four servant songs of Isaiah, in which the Servant alternately functions as Israel, the Messiah, or both. See *The Book of Isaiah* by Jim McGuiggan.[4]
- Wisdom and Sirach (next entry) are heavily cited in the patristic writers.

Sirach (Ecclesiasticus)

- Sirach is the only apocryphal book whose author's name is known.
- The oldest manuscript is a fragment found at Qumran (the famous Dead Sea community) in 1952—nearly two millennia old.
- Allusions to Sirach are possibly found in the book of James (for example, Sirach 2:1 in James 1:2-4 and 1:12-15; Sirach 2:3 in James 5:7-8; Sirach 5:11 in James 1:19, etc.) and in the Sermon on the Mount (Sirach 7:14 in Matthew 6:7).
- Yet, not everything is theologically correct—12:4-7 teaches the opposite of Luke 6:27-31 (don't give to the unrighteous). In 25:24-26 we read that we may divorce a wife if we are having marriage problems. And in 30:1 we read, "He who loves his son will whip him often...." Although it is similar to the teaching of Proverbs, it goes just a bit too far, doesn't it?

- Good advice is found for stock investors in 31:1—"Wakefulness over wealth wastes away one's flesh, and anxiety about it removes sleep."
- In chapters 31-32 we find extensive advice on etiquette, including table manners!
- In 33:24-31, 42:5 the treatment of slaves comes to the fore: "[Do not be ashamed...] of whipping a wicked servant severely" and "Yoke and thong will bow the neck, and for a wicked servant there are racks and tortures" (33:26—yikes!).
- In 50:25-26 anti-Edomite and anti-Samaritan prejudice are extreme.

> With two nations my soul is vexed, and the third is no
> nation: Those who live on Mount Seir, and the Philistines,
> and the foolish people that dwell in Shechem.

- To sum up: He is a theologian of rank, and a teacher of religious truth, but nonetheless a man of the world, proud of his practical philosophy. Put your trust in the Lord (32:24, 33:1), but trust also the wisdom that comes of experience. His advice to the sick man, 38:1-15, may serve for partial illustration.

> My son, when you are ill pray to the Lord, and he will heal
> you. Cleanse your heart from sin, offer your sacrifice, and
> then put yourself in the hands of a physician, for God created
> him (this is said twice), let him not go from you. A
> wise man will not refuse to take medicines. (Torrey, *The
> Apocryphal Literature,* 94)

Baruch

- Though pretending to be written by Jeremiah's secretary, this short work, Baruch, was written in the second or first century BC—three or four centuries too late.

Letter of Jeremiah

- Like Baruch, the Letter of Jeremiah also appears with the canonical Jeremiah.
- This is a polemic against idolatry and was written fourth to second century BC.
- The oldest surviving manuscript was found at Qumran and dates from 100 BC.

Song of the Three

- The three are Shadrach, Meshach and Abednego, and in this add-on to Daniel we find embellishments galore, as the three wax eloquent while strolling about in the fire.

Susanna

- In the Septuagint and Vulgate, Susanna is Daniel 13 in the Apocrypha.

Bel and the Dragon

- Another add-on to Daniel, Bel (the Babylonian god) and the Dragon teaches (incorrectly) that those who worship God will be preserved through every trial. The theology is reminiscent of that of Eliphaz, Bildad and Zophar in Job's day or that of the pious people and priests in Jesus' day (Matthew 27:41-43).
- Stunningly, in verse 33 the prophet Habakkuk is still alive.
- One final blooper: in verses 31 and 40, Daniel has been in the lions' den for seven days, not just on an overnighter as in the canonical Daniel. Oh, well!

Prayer of Manasseh

- The Prayer of Manasseh is a stirring, humble prayer, though only rarely appearing in the Apocrypha. The wicked king Manasseh—who did indeed repent in the OT account—pours out his heart.
- One problem: It is claimed that Abraham, Isaac and Jacob did not sin against God (v8).

1 Maccabees

- Written in the second century BC, this book is extremely valuable for filling in the gaps in our understanding of Israel's history. Furthermore, for the second century, it is our only source.
- Facing the Hellenistic challenge—the pressure to eat pork, embrace idolatry, violate the Sabbath, "uncircumcise" themselves, etc.—the faithful admirably resist.

> But many in Israel stood firm and were resolved in their hearts not to eat unclean food. They chose to die rather than to be defiled by food or to profane the holy covenant; and they did die (1 Maccabees 1:62-63).

- The Romans are flattered in a way to make Luke shudder. In 8:14-16, it is claimed that the Romans don't struggle with pride!
- In 13:22 we read of a heavy snow. It does occasionally snow in Israel, and occasionally we find meteorological insights in the apocryphal writings.
- Finally, for the reader of Daniel 10-12, 1-2 Maccabees supplies the necessary intertestamental details, picturing the resistance of the people of God against dominating, "Hellenizing" Greeks.

2 Maccabees

- Composed around 100 BC, 2 Maccabees is a jazzed-up version of 1 Maccabees 1:10-7:50.
- The most famous section is the story of the martyrdom of the seven brothers and their mother, which is found in chapter 7. This in fact is the subject of 4 Maccabees.
- In 12:43-45 we find approval of prayer and sacrifices for the dead and in 15:14-16, intercessory prayer for the dead.
- As with the Apocrypha in general, there is no, "Thus says the Lord." Consider 15:37c-38: "So I too will here end my story. If it is well told and to the point, that is what I myself desired; if it is poorly done and mediocre, that was the best I could do." Such "insecurity statements" are typical not only of the Apocrypha, but of most religious scriptures outside the Bible.

3 Maccabees

- Set in the third century BC, long before the Maccabean period, the name of the book, "3 Maccabees," is a real misnomer. The situation is somewhat similar to the second century Maccabean one: a pagan king is persecuting Jews. It was probably written in the first century BC.
- 3 Maccabees represents Orthodox Judaism.

4 Maccabees

- 4 Maccabees was written in AD 20-54, possibly during the reign of Caligula (37-41).
- Though never canonized, 4 Maccabees was influential in the Eastern churches.

- The thesis is that reason can control the emotions. This book is a philosophical piece based on 2 Maccabees 6:12-7:42 (the martyrdom of the seven brothers).
- A more suitable title would be, "The Apocalypse of Shealtiel."
- In 1:11, 17:21 and 18:4 we find the substitutionary atonement of martyrs.
- In 7:19 and 16:25 the martyrs are immediately immortal.

Psalm 151

- Psalm 151 is found in the Greek LXX.
- It also appears in several other ancient versions: Old Latin, Syriac, Armenian, Ethiopic and Arabic.
- An expanded version of Psalm 151 was found at Qumran in Cave 11.

Lingering Questions

Before we conclude this study, there are a couple of unanswered questions which may be fruitful to explore. First of all, if the LXX contained the Apocrypha and the Greek-speaking church used the LXX as their Old Testament, does this not mean that they accepted the inspiration of the Apocrypha?

It is true that the LXX contains the Apocrypha, except for 2 Esdras.[5] This being the case, it is certain that the early Christians were familiar with the Apocrypha, and we have already considered evidence that this is the case. Whether or not certain disciples considered the Apocrypha to be inspired is one matter; whether God in his word has clarified that they are inspired is quite another. It remains to ask why these books are never once quoted from in the New Testament if they are part of God's revelation to us.

Another question is, "Why are the Apocrypha not in the Hebrew Bible?" After 70 AD, as you know, with the temple and its cultus dismantled, the Jews turned to the study of Torah. A fierce concern grew that no other writings should even appear to be on a par with the most sacred books.

Moreover, the Christians were circulating more and more Hebrew and Aramaic writings, some of which cogently supported the new faith. The Christian reliance on the Semitic texts actually catalyzed the Jews to define their own canon. For example, Wisdom 2:12-3:9 is often quoted by early Christians as they set out proofs that the Righteous One, the Messiah, would be rejected by the religious establishment. Probably this is why Rabbi Akiba said, "Among those who have no part in the world to come is he who reads the outside books" (Jerusalem *Sanhedrin*, x, 1, fol. 28a; also Babylonian *Sanhedrin*, 100b). And Gamaliel II, around 80 AD, pronounced an anathema on the Christians (virtually including their books and any who should read them). The result of these "anti-apocryphal" factors was a systematic destruction of the disturbing books. This meant the Semitic originals of all extra-canonical literature, not only the Christian writings, but also the Apocrypha which the Christians were using. (Similarly, only two of Tyndale's six thousand Bibles survived the Biblical purge of the 1500s.)

"Whosoever brings together in his house more than twenty-four books (the canonical thirty-nine books as grouped by the Jews) brings confusion" (*Midrash Qoheleth*, 12, 12). And so Jewish popular literature no longer flourished. Ironically, as the Jews relinquished their own popular literature (the Apocrypha), the Christians were increasingly making use of it in their own apologetics, worship and study.

Conclusion

The Apocrypha are certainly useful reading for understanding what happened between the end of canonical OT times (the 400s BC) and the beginning of the NT times (first century AD). As Torrey rightly says,

> Acquaintance with the Jewish uncanonical religious writings of the pre-Christian period is now generally recognized as belonging to the equipment of every serious student of the Bible, in either Testament, for they throw light in both directions. (*The Apocryphal Literature*, v)

I highly recommend that men and women of the Book read the Apocrypha—at least once—and this is one reason this study has been written. It never hurts to be informed.

Do these books have any authority of their own? There is no, "Thus says the Lord" anywhere, in sharp contrast to the books of the Old Testament and New Testament, which are replete with authority statements. As someone put it, when you are driving along the highway, it helps to see clearly the road signs put there to help you on your journey. Whereas the Old Testament and New Testament frequently provide such helpful signs, the "outside books" do not. The Apocrypha lack the decisive "Thus says the Lord."

It is indeed true that the Apocrypha makes no claim to inspiration. Yet sometimes weak arguments against the inspiration of the Apocrypha have been elaborated. (I myself have done so in the past.) Passages like 1 Maccabees 4:46, 9:27, 14:41 and Song of the Three (verse 15) are cited, passages which mention the passing of the age of prophecy. But since when is prophecy the essential criterion for legitimate Scripture? In Psalm 74:9 and Lamentations 2:9 the "voice of prophecy" has been silenced, but if that means the document in which this lament is found is not inspired, then Psalms and Lamentations must be merely of man and not of God.

The nub of the issue is the *error* of the Apocrypha; amidst all the good, there is the bad. Amidst the precious and even the "inspiring," there is the dross. How different from the canonical Scriptures: "And the words of the Lord are flawless, like silver refined in a furnace of clay, purified seven times" (Psalm 12:6).

Still, it remains that the Apocrypha is good reading. The thinking disciple ought not to fear that this admission is a concession to inspiration. The popular *Chicken Soup for the Soul* books, often quoted and bandied about on the Internet these days, make for inspiring reading, and yet they are not inspired either. In short, "inspiring" does not mean "inspired."

The Bible is crystal clear that we are not to entertain any additions to the Word (Deuteronomy 4:2, 12:32, Proverbs 30:6, 1 Corinthians 4:6, Galatians 1:6-9, Revelation 22:18-19). Despite this plain Biblical truth, many appeal to the Apocrypha or to other extra-Biblical works to justify their beliefs. These apocryphal writings attempt to touch on areas not covered in the Scriptures, as well as to improve on the revelation God has given to his people. As Paul wrote, "learn...the meaning of the saying, 'Do not go beyond what is written'" (1 Corinthians 4:6).

The early church ended up accepting the authority and inspiration of the Apocrypha. The Reformation attempted (partially) to remedy the error, while the Counter-Reformation entrenched itself and elevated the outside writings to inspired status. We are wrong if we continue to preach, "The Catholic Church added the Apocrypha to their Bibles in 1546," for, practically speaking, it for centuries had been a part of their Bible. Quite the opposite: Protestants were beginning to remove it, though they did not succeed for another three hundred years. And if we learn the lessons that emerge from our study of church history—with all the ambivalence toward outside writings—then we may avoid the proven pitfalls of adding to the Word.

Finally, a word for you who have the Apocrypha in your Bibles. How should you view this addition? Most of us have "helps" in the back pages of our Bibles: tables of weights and measures, maps, even reference notes. This material is useful, but not inspired. In the same way that we may grow rather fond of the extra material at the end of our Bibles, so the early church grew fond of the extra material in their books. In time, the mistake was made of elevating it to virtually inspired status.

So, benefit from these materials, *if* you are so inclined and *if* you have already read the entire true Bible through. (I usually recommend that until someone has read the entire Old Testament at least three or four times, he should stay away from the extra writings.)

Don't be confused: The Apocrypha are not inspired.

Notes

[1] Check *The Ante-Nicene Fathers, Vols. 1-9* (Peabody, Mass.: Hendrickson, 1994).

[2] James H. Charlesworth, ed., *The Old Testament Pseudepigrapha*, Vols. 1-2 (New York: Doubleday, 1983).

[3] Also helpful are Philip Wesley Comfort, ed., *The Origin of the Bible* (Wheaton: Tyndale, 1992), Neil Lightfoot, *How We Got the Bible, 2nd ed.*, (Grand Rapids: Baker, 1994) and Charles Cutter Torrey, *The Apocryphal Literature: A Brief Introduction* (London: Archon Books, 1945).

[4] Jim McGuiggan, *The Book of Isaiah* (Fort Worth: Star Bible Publications, 1985), phone: 1-800-433-7507.

[5] Note: the Vulgate usually included both 1 and 2 Esdras, although, as noted, these books are no longer found in the OT section of Catholic Bibles.

5
Musical Instruments in Worship

Instrumental Music: A Live Issue

—September 1993

This paper is an expansion of a lesson taught in London in 1984. At that time my conclusion was that instrumental music (IM), though not a truly doctrinal issue as such, was best kept out of the church. My thinking has developed during the past decade, though the basic premise of the paper has not. I hope this contribution will be helpful in our current musical discussion.

Who would have thought that IM was a damnable sin? Not me! I remember well my first retreat in October 1977. At a class on the Restoration Movement, a well-meaning man offered the following analogy:

> Suppose you paid a man to come to pave your driveway. How would you feel if he paved your garden too? You wouldn't be too happy, would you? No. Why not? Because you hadn't authorized him to pave your garden. He had no authority to do it. We need authority for every practice we follow, and instrumental music has no authority in the New Testament.

So the argument went. The ultimate conclusion: any teaching or practice not specifically "authorized" by the New Testament was damnable. Only the Church of Christ teaches the truth on IM, hence it's the true church. (Fortunately repentance and baptism were also taught and, despite the doctrinally questionable teaching on IM, the next day I was baptized.)

Today, sixteen years later, we are reevaluating this issue in our movement, the International Churches of Christ. Is IM really a doctrinal issue? Is it prohibited, commanded or only tolerated? Do the Scriptures speak clearly on this subject, or is it one of those gray areas? These are the questions this paper addresses itself to. The outline is simple; the paper brief:

1. Theoretical Underpinnings
2. Historical Overview
3. Scriptural Interpretation
4. Linguistic Illumination
5. Conclusion

Of course, it should be understood that the discussion concerns IM in the assembly, since for years we've had IM at concerts and other special events. And now, let's begin.

Theoretical Underpinnings

What is the thinking behind a theology that forbids music, missionary societies and kitchens in the church building? Much has been said lately about the pithy proverb: Speak where the Bible speaks; be silent where the Bible is silent. Properly understood and applied, this gives us great freedom. Yet in the Restoration Movement, especially over the course of the nineteenth century, the saying was inverted. Instead of being led into glorious freedom, the movement was led astray into increasingly inglorious legalism. Our lawyers were very good, every bit as clever as the Jewish rabbis who expounded on the Law.

Nadab & Abihu, Inc.

A classic proof text used in the Restoration Movement was Leviticus 10:1-2:

> Aaron's sons Nadab and Abihu took their censers, put fire in them and added incense; and they offered unauthorized fire before the Lord, contrary to his command. So fire came out from the presence of the Lord and consumed them, and they died before the Lord. (Leviticus 10:1-2)

Nadab and Abihu were struck dead for their irreverent act of offering unauthorized fire to the Lord. Imagine the gall, to improvise like that! Never mind that a specific command had been broken (Exodus 30:9), proving that disobedience and not improvisation was the real cause of God's anger.

Patternism

"Patternism" is the conviction that there's a pattern for everything and that just as Moses was to follow the pattern shown him on the mountain (Exodus 25:40), so we, under the New Covenant, must discover and adhere strictly to the pattern—the pattern for worship, leadership and everything else. Of course, patternism includes two questionable assumptions: (1) that a "pattern" exists and (2) that we have found the correct pattern. One is never allowed the luxury of being wrong, since to deviate from the pattern is to be lost, and salvation is dependent on the pattern. Sadly, from 1860 on, it was generally assumed in the Restoration Movement that the "New Testament church" had been restored. And since the NT "pattern" didn't mention IM, it must be forbidden. Such is the theory, at any rate. Given such an approach to Scripture (and to God), it isn't surprising that IM became such a focal point for controversy.

Historical Overview

Next, let's trace the development of attitudes toward IM through the centuries. As you'll see from the table on the following page, IM is quite rare in earliest and latest times, though in the broad, fuzzy middle period, it played a major role in worship.

Thus, we see that historically our movement has avoided the use of IM. This in itself, however, is no argument against IM. The issue, if truly a doctrinal one, must be informed by the Bible. And so on to the next section.

Scriptural Interpretation

We've already seen how Leviticus 10 has been misused to uphold a patternistic approach to interpretation. Yet, there are many more passages whose examination will prove helpful to our inquiry. Consider how strong the case against IM is after perusing these Scriptures.

Numbers 20

Moses, having been told to speak to the rock, actually struck the rock with his staff. Was Moses bound to perfect obedience before the blessing (water) came? Even though Moses, in the heat of emotion, technically disobeyed God by striking the rock, the blessing came anyway. Patternists are of the opinion that he should keep going back until he "got it right." Thus, his spiritual attitude is of little account.

Historical Dates in Relation to Instrumental Music

Developments	*Year (AD)*	*Notes*
No instrumental music—church follows Jewish synagogue practice, against that of pagan Mystery Religions, which nearly always used instruments to accompany their idolatrous and sensual religious rites.	30 -100	Apparent unity of practice throughout the first century. In the second century, it was often illegal to practice the faith. It is easy to see why worship would avoid noisy instruments.
Christianity becomes the official religion of the Roman Empire. Jewish and pagan elements infiltrate the church at an alarming rate.	381	Eighty years earlier, Christianity had become legal Empire-wide.
Introduction of music is more common. Also at this time, the Great Apostasy sees intensification of moral and spiritual demise of the faith.	400?	The Church splits, East and West. There is argument over the true leader of the church.
Organs are first used.	900	
The Catholic-Orthodox split is now irreparable. The corruption of the traditional church is soon to reach its worst depths.	1054	
The Protestant Reformation begins with Martin Luther in Germany. Many reformers stood opposed to IM. For instance, the Anabaptists favored a cappella singing (1524). Calvin also stood opposed.	1517	
The first "Church of Christ" in Scotland: eldership, adult baptism, name "Church of Christ," weekly Lord's Supper, a cappella singing—it was Calvinistic and nonevangelistic.	1690	The Restoration Movement starts within Scotch Baptist churches and moves down in England and across America by the early 1800s.
"Instrument" introduced at Midway, Kentucky. Interestingly, the most ardent advocates insisted that IM wasn't a term of fellowship.	1859	In favor of the organ: "The singing [a cappella] was so deplorable it scared the rats away!"
Death of Alexander Campbell—before this, controversies tended to be rather low-key. After this, things heat up considerably!	1866	Campbell's influence dominated the American movement through most of the nineteenth century.
Britons (tended to be more conservative) criticize Americans over use of instruments.	1868	
The Churches of Christ first differentiated from the Christian Church. This is my position after poring over contemporary issues of *British Millennial Harbinger* at the British Library in London.	1889	
There was discord over instruments, and there were lawsuits, ending four decades of disagreement without division.	1890s	The Church of Christ was truly an issues oriented group.
US Census: Churches of Christ were considered a separate denomination. Most were anti-instrumental.	1906	IM was not a major issue; there were many others!

Another passage which shows God's grace and flexibility is 2 Chronicles 30:20. Ritual law is never as important as moral law.

2 Chronicles 29:25

Often it's said that in the Old Testament, IM was allowed, but never commanded. This could hardly be further from the truth. In this passage we see that instrumental music wasn't just David's idea; it was commanded by God.

> He stationed the Levites in the temple of the Lord with cymbals, harps and lyres in the way prescribed by David and Gad the king's seer and Nathan the prophet; this was commanded by the Lord through his prophets. (2 Chronicles 29:25)

The passage speaks for itself. True, the command isn't repeated in the New Testament, but that doesn't necessarily invalidate it. (It didn't make the hit list in Colossians 2:15-16.) Nor can one reason the other way: bestiality is forbidden in the Old Testament (Leviticus 18), but the absence of a prohibition in the New Testament in no way means it's allowed. The question may be asked, "Is it commanded today?" For reasons to be set forth in a moment, we may answer a solid no—but this in no way means it is prohibited. How can you prove that this is an issue or test of fellowship?

The Psalms

Singing is enjoined upon the saints in the Old Testament: Psalm 42:8, 47:7, 77:6, 101:1. But so is IM. (See Psalm 49:4, 57:7-8, 108:1-2, 71:22, 92:2-3 and 150:3-5.) One could sum up with a verse in the Psalter that flatly says that instrumental music is "good":

> It is good to praise the LORD
>   and make music to your name, O Most High,
> to proclaim your love in the morning
>   and your faithfulness at night,
> to the music of the ten-stringed lyre
>   and the melody of the harp. (Psalm 92:1-3)

If it is "good," then we really should have no problem with it.

Then there are the musical directions at the heads of many psalms. A catalogue may be tedious, but something can definitely be learned. We see different classes of instruction.

- Stringed instruments: 4, 6, 54-55, 61, 67, 76.
- "For the director of music": 8-9, 11-14, 18-22, 31, 36, 39-42, 44-47, 49, 51-53, 56-59, 62, 64-66, 68-70, 75, 77, 80-81, 84-85, 88, 109, 139-140.
- "Psalm" (a musical term itself): 3-6, 8-9, 12-13, 15, 19-24, 29-31, 38-41, 47-51, 62-68, 73, 75-77, 79-80, 82-85, 87-88, 92, 98, 100-101, 108-110, 139-141, 143.
- Flutes: 5.

In light of the huge number of verses giving commands and instruction for IM in Psalms alone, it's difficult to see how anyone could say God only "tolerated" it in OT times—as he "tolerated" writs of divorce (Deuteronomy 24).

Amos 6:5

A scathing denouncement of complacent worshipers, often taken as a rebuke for using IM, is found in Amos 6:5:

> You strum away on your harps like David
> and improvise on musical instruments.

But in context, Amos isn't criticizing them for using IM, but rather for being nonchalant toward the cause of righteousness. (A NT parallel may be found in Revelation 18:22.)

Ephesians 5:19

The New Testament contains no specific commands to use IM as such, though perhaps Ephesians 5:19 comes closest to "authorizing" it: "Speak to one another with psalms, hymns and spiritual songs. Sing and make music in your heart to God." The word translated as "make music" is the same root word translated as "psalms" in the previous sentence. This makes it extremely difficult to interpret psalms in a strictly instrumental way. (If that were the case, strictly speaking, we would have to keep the [instrumental] music in our hearts.)

In fact, "psalm" has several possible meanings:

- sacred song accompanied by a stringed instrument (not the usual meaning)
- the words of the sacred song, without reference to accompaniment

- the words of the song as a piece of Scripture, again without musical reference (the normal meaning we encounter in the New Testament)
- possibly, the tune to which such a song is sung or played

Which meaning is in mind must be understood from the context, and since "speech" is what Paul has in mind in Ephesians 5:19, it would appear he's using the term in a neutral or even noninstrumental way. This brings us to a more serious consideration of the linguistic background of the ancient word we translate as "psalm."

Linguistic Illumination

Here are some of the basic Hebrew and Greek words in the "psalm" family.

Hebrew:

- *Zimrah* = music piece or psalm to be accompanied by an instrument; melody; psalm.
- *Mizmor* = instrumental music; by implication, a poem set to notes. OT psalms are clearly set to music.

Greek:

- *Psallo* = pluck; sing
- *Psalmos* = twang; tune, song. My position is that *psalmos* in the New Testament did not mean anything necessarily instrumental.

Classical Greek

The nonspecialist may tend to lump all Greek together, but in fact the Greek language is much older than the classical Greek we may have heard of. Attic Greek, the dialect of Athenians at the high point of their culture (400s and 300s BC), became the standard for classical Greek, but by NT times the language had changed significantly. The common language of NT times was called Koine Greek. Modern Greek is entirely different again.

To lump them all together is overly simplistic. You might as well assume an English word in the 900s (Old English) kept its meaning in the 1300s (Middle English), and even in the 1600s (Modern English). The King James translation, which is difficult for nearly all English speakers to grasp well, is actually a specimen of Modern

English—not Old English. For instance, in the King James Version, "conversation" means not speech or dialogue, but conduct. And most readers of this paper are wholly unable to understand Old or Middle English (me included)!

In ancient Greek *psallo*, meant "to touch, stir or move by touching; to pull, pluck; to pull and let go again, twang with the fingers." In the absolute, it meant "to play" and later "to sing to a harp."[1] The instrumental connotation is unmistakable.

Septuagint Greek

In the third century BC, the Hebrew Old Testament was translated into Greek for the benefit of Jews no longer familiar or comfortable with the mother tongue. It's interesting to see how certain words were rendered into this translation into Greek.

For example, the Hebrew *rosh* means "head." In Septuagintal Greek, this word is most often translated *kephale*. When we hear the word "head," we think of the body part first, then the meaning of head as "ruler." But when *rosh* means head in the sense of "ruler," it's regularly rendered *archon*. When *rosh* is translated *kephale*, in nearly every case it means "head" in the sense of "source" (as in the "head" of a river), and not "head" in the sense of "ruler." This throws light on 1 Corinthians 11, where man is the "head" (*kephale*, not *archon*) of woman. How many of us knew that? How could you unless you were a student of Greek? Words change meaning— exactly the point in connection with *psallo*.

In translation Greek *psallo* usually does not mean "to play," but rather "to sing." This is a few centuries before Paul wrote Ephesians.[2]

New Testament (Koine) Greek

In the Greek New Testament the only documents even approaching classical Greek are Hebrews, Luke and Acts. Hebrews is the finest specimen. Next, Luke's two works have the finest Greek. The early portion of Luke is deliberately written in a Septuagintal style, probably to give the lead-up to the ministry of Jesus an old-time feel. But on the whole, NT Greek had changed considerably since classical times. One instance is the word *psallo*. In NT Greek it means to "sing" or "sing praise." There is, in my opinion, a remote chance that it means to sing to stringed accompaniment, but I wouldn't put any money on it.

Modern Greek

In the modern Greek language *psallo* means to "sing" exclusively. It has nothing whatsoever to do with instrumental accompaniment.

Summary

It would seem that there's no justification (from Ephesians 5) for the position that the New Testament commands IM. The most we can say is that there is a dearth of evidence. And since it isn't disallowed, it is safe to teach that it's allowed.

Conclusion

While IM was definitely commanded in OT worship, it isn't commanded in the New Testament. The early church closely followed synagogue practice (as against large-scale, instrumental temple worship), which was small-scale and noninstrumental. Centuries of reluctance to assimilate Christianity to pagan religions (first), plus patternistic exegesis in reaction against denominational error (later), led to its rejection, even though there were no scriptural grounds for such a position. Specious linguistic arguments have been enlisted on both sides of the controversy. IM requires no NT authorization; its implementation is a practical question, not primarily a Biblical one.

In short, here are the conclusions of this essay:

- Instrumental music is neither commanded nor prohibited by the New Testament.
- There's no convincing proof that we stand under the OT command to have IM.
- This is thus an area of Christian liberty.
- So, to the extent that IM expedites the gospel, we should be willing to use it.

Notes

[1] Source: Liddell & Scott, *Greek-English Lexicon*.

[2] Walter Bauer, *Greek-English Lexicon of the New Testament and other Early Christian Literature* (Chicago: University of Chicago Press, 1957).

Who Are We?

Discipleship Publications International (DPI) began publishing in 1993. We are a nonprofit Christian publisher affiliated with the International Churches of Christ, committed to publishing and distributing materials that honor God, lift up Jesus Christ and show how his message practically applies to all areas of life. We have a deep conviction that no one changes life like Jesus and that the implementation of his teaching will revolutionize any life, any marriage, any family and any singles household.

Since our beginning, we have published more than 100 titles; plus, we have produced a number of important, spiritual audio products. More than one million volumes have been printed, and our works have been translated into more than a dozen languages—international is not just a part of our name! Our books are shipped regularly to every inhabited continent.

To see a more detailed description of our works, find us on the World Wide Web at www.dpibooks.org. You can order books by calling 1-888-DPI-BOOK twenty-four hours a day.

We appreciate the hundreds of comments we have received from readers. We would love to hear from you. Here are other ways to get in touch:

Mail: DPI, 2 Sterling Road, Billerica, MA 01862-2595
E-Mail: dpibooks@icoc.org

Find Us on the World Wide Web

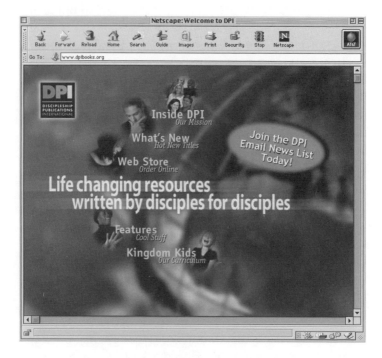

www.dpibooks.org
1-888-DPI-BOOK